LGC: The making of a company

From government agency
to international business

Richard Worswick

Carrick Press

British Library Cataloguing in Publication Data.
A CIP catalogue record for this book is available
from the British Library.

ISBN 978-0-9569553-0-2

Typeset by TechType, Abingdon, Oxon OX14 3SX
Printed and bound by CPI Group (UK) Ltd, Croydon, CR0 4YY

Carrick Press
Abingdon, Oxon

www.lgcthemakingofacompany.com

Contents

Introduction

The UK privatisations which began under the Conservative government in the 1980s changed the political and industrial landscape fundamentally. The sale of state interests in telecommunications, gas, electricity, water, an airline, airports, railways, ports, and nuclear energy was a radical policy. The model of privatisation varied widely. Some state enterprises operated in competitive markets or markets with the potential to open up. For these, deregulation and full exposure to competition (rather than change in ownership *per se*) drove productivity and customer service improvements. Although their overall performance in relation to their competitors has not been remarkable, no-one would today seriously argue that BT and BA are not better sitting in the private sector than if they had remained as nationalised companies.

The situation for monopoly providers, such as utilities, was different. In some cases it was possible to introduce elements of competition into their markets, but it generally required oversight by independent regulators to drive efficiency improvements and lower prices for consumers. Some UK utility companies were lured by the temptation to escape the control of the regulator and threw money at acquisitions in non-regulated sectors at home and overseas – the relatively comfortable process of meeting investment bankers, rather than the challenging task of addressing consumer and operational concerns. The results of such diversification were often poor. Few of the initial privatisation structures for utility companies remain today. Occasionally, in the case of the ill-considered privatisation of the railways for example, the state has been required to step back in. In general, and perhaps inevitably, the ownership structure which at privatisation began with widespread public share ownership has now reverted to the typical plc situation of ownership by pension funds, insurance companies or overseas parents.

However, it is not so much the performance of individual businesses or indeed their initial ownership structure, but rather the major cultural changes brought about by these privatisations which is the lasting legacy of a policy which has been adopted throughout the world and which no political party in the UK now suggests reversing. Because they were ultimately accountable for them, politicians of all political persuasions, and civil servants acting on their behalf, were always tempted, and expected, to intervene in the management of state-owned bodies. Used as instruments of political or public policy, such bodies were very hard to run. Only by transferring ownership of their assets was it possible to achieve the partial or full disengagement of the state. Operating in the private sector, managers of these companies were able to concentrate on running their businesses. Some have done it well, others badly.

Pressure on the UK science budget led to calls in the 1990s for the rationalisation of government scientific establishments. Providing important scientific services, these bodies perhaps had something in common with utilities, but they were not obvious candidates for privatisation. However, following reviews initiated by the Rt Hon Michael Heseltine when he was President of the Board of Trade, those scientific agencies owned by the Department of Trade and Industry (DTI) were transferred in various ways to private ownership in the final period of the Conservative government. The Laboratory of the Government Chemist, sold in 1996, was one of the last to be privatised, and possibly the least expected, partly because of the historic role of the Government Chemist. Unlike the science-based companies Amersham plc (the first of the 1980 privatisations) and AEA Technology plc, which moved to the private sector through interim stages as trading funds, the Laboratory of the Government Chemist had very little commercial track record. Although it had able scientific staff, it was not clear how the laboratory could manage outside government and, at the time, the risks seemed high. Nevertheless, I believed its scientific work was important and should be safeguarded and, moreover, that the organisation had the potential to develop as a business. When, after DTI had carefully considered all options, the Laboratory of the Government Chemist was put up for sale, I decided to form a consortium to bid to buy it. This led to a unique management buy-out from a central government department. Over the following 15 years, the company has been hugely successful. It is now an international business with laboratories and offices in over 20 countries, a staff of 1,300 and an annual turnover ten times what it was at the point of privatisation.

Many privatisations were of unwieldy public bodies where change involved cuts in costs and reduction in staffing. LGC's launch into the private sector was different. The organisation was relatively small and I had already restructured it extensively during its period as a government Agency. Building a new company from the core transferred from government was a highly creative task and provided the opportunity for me to put into practice some of my management philosophy. The key challenge was rapidly to change the focus of the organisation and pursue opportunities in new markets. My desire for widespread staff share ownership helped foster a partnership approach throughout an organisation which was staffed predominantly by highly qualified people, interested primarily in their work rather than in the challenge of creating a business.

The company culture I tried to foster was one of mutual respect and support, with a strong customer focus. It emphasised the importance of sound science, quality, and integrity, but also encouraged entrepreneurship and innovation. It concentrated on building a sound business over the longer term rather than rapid shareholder returns. The leadership team I built up over time was not a collection of clones; drawing on heterogeneous skills, even if at times it created tensions, led to more creative approaches. The type of leadership I encouraged, while demanding decisiveness and direction, drew out strengths and addressed weaknesses through discussion and consideration of options, rather than resorting to macho aggression. Much of the work we undertook – for example, in ensuring the safety of food and medicines, in providing forensic services to the police, in establishing an international framework for chemical measurements and standards – underpinned the safety and security of the public, and we took our responsibilities to the wider community seriously. LGC was a company with a role we could all be proud of, and social as well as financial considerations played a part in the company's development. Its remarkable growth could not have been achieved had it remained in the public sector.

I have frequently been asked about the background to LGC's privatisation and how the new company, with little previous experience of operating in competitive markets, developed in the way it did. My purpose in writing this book is to describe the period as an Agency of DTI leading up to privatisation, my decision to bid to buy the Laboratory, and the subsequent development of LGC, the company. It is primarily a narrative about the company, which I hope will be of interest to those who were involved.

However, I hope it may also be helpful to those considering the challenges of privatisation, as well as those involved in building businesses based on science. There are aspects of LGC's story which may have some relevance to those planning or working in the field of social enterprise.

I am grateful to those who have helped me in the preparation of this book. Dr John Marriott kindly read the text and made helpful comments. Likewise, Nicholas Clarke and Geoff Battersby looked at specific parts of the text and suggested some changes and corrections. I should also particularly like to thank Lorna Hopkinson-Hall, my former PA, who has diligently searched for information which I knew existed but could not find, has sorted through and transported boxes of papers, and has checked some key names and dates which I could not recall. Sarah Davey, Claire Whitley and Debbie Grafetsberger dug out documents and photographs which enabled me to check my own notes and records. I should also like to thank Andrew Brooks who took many of the photographs in the book and helped assemble them for publication. I am also grateful to Mark Thornton who advised on, and managed, publication.

I owe an immeasurable debt of gratitude to my wife, Jacqueline. Quite simply, without her support LGC would not exist in the form it does today. She encouraged me to accept the job leading a Next Steps Agency, knowing that even more of the burden of caring for our very ill eldest daughter would fall on her; she urged me to go ahead with my management buy-out, despite the financial risk; and she played a very significant, if rather hidden, role in some of the key stages in LGC's development. She has acted as editor, adviser and proof reader for this book, and her incredible memory has prompted me to include things that I had almost forgotten. I am very fortunate to have such a wonderfully supportive partner, from whom I have been able to tap wisdom and creativity.

LGC's success was rooted in the team efforts of its staff, and I will forever be grateful for their support during my management buy-out and over the years that followed. I have been extremely fortunate in working with people who enjoyed their work, and were excited at the opportunity to help shape the company. Some of them I have mentioned in this book, but it has obviously not been possible to name the many colleagues who worked tirelessly to make a success of our company. This book is dedicated to the staff of LGC who helped make the company what it is today.

Chapter 1: *The Agency years*

The birth of a new company – The origins of The Laboratory of the Government Chemist – Being part of the civil service – 150th anniversary celebrations – Evolution of Next Steps Agencies – Rationalising the delivery of government science – Starting to make changes

Sunday 31st March 1996 certainly marked a turning point in my life. Although my wife, Jacqueline, and I and our three daughters spent a quiet and uneventful day at home, I was waiting for a rather unusual phone call from John Hobday, a senior civil servant at the Department of Trade and Industry. The phone call duly came that evening; 'Just checking that you're alive and well', said John.

I had returned to our home in Abingdon late on the previous Friday night, having signed a vast number of agreements which would enable the company that I had formed to buy the Laboratory of the Government Chemist from the Government. The deal was to come into force at midnight on Sunday and it would have been a legal minefield had I not survived the period between the signing on the Friday and midnight on Sunday 31st. So John Hobday was relieved to hear that I was still extant, and after the call I set off late to stay the night in my flat next to the Laboratory in Teddington so that I could arrive at my desk early the following morning as head of the newly privatised LGC.

Although I had ambitions for the new company, I could not know then how it would develop over the next decade into such a successful and entrepreneurial science-based company, with offices and laboratories throughout Europe and in India, and a foothold in the US. I was completely in charge, and the freedom I had in leading and shaping my own company was tremendously invigorating, particularly after the interesting but rather stifling period I had spent in the civil service. I was immensely fortunate to be able to lead, mould and develop my own company; it was a unique opportunity to put my management beliefs into practice.

I had joined the Laboratory of the Government Chemist as its chief executive on 29th April 1991 and at the same time had been appointed Government Chemist. The Laboratory had only recently become a Next Steps Agency of the Department of Trade and Industry (in October 1989). It had just completed a laborious move from temporary premises (where it had been for 25 years!) in Cornwall House, Waterloo to splendid new laboratories in Teddington which were formally opened by Alan Clark, Minister for Trade on 10th July 1989 (though, unaccountably, this is not an event that is a major feature of his diaries).

I was appointed to run this new Agency from outside the civil service, as a result of the relatively recent reforms which allowed for senior civil service posts to be filled through 'open competition'. I had been interviewed in a dark building in Whitehall by a 'board', chaired by the First Civil Service Commissioner, Mr John Holroyd, and a roomful of other interviewers including Dr Ron Coleman, the chief engineer and scientist at the Department of Trade and Industry (DTI), who were arranged in a horseshoe around the candidate. The ordeal, during which questions were fired from all directions, lasted just 45 minutes – an extraordinary way of making such appointments – but evidently my performance was better than that of the other five shortlisted candidates being interviewed that day, whose names I was able to see on the clipboard of the woman who took me to the interview room.

Next Steps Agencies were part of the quiet reform in the civil service which resulted from the Ibbs Report of 1988 *Improving Management in Government: The Next Steps*. The aim was to create Executive Agencies within government departments which would undertake the executive functions of the government (as opposed to policy advice) and foster a culture of efficiency, effectiveness and value for money. These Agencies were managed by chief executives who would report directly to ministers and, although remaining as senior civil servants, would be given new freedoms within a 'policy and resources framework' agreed between the Agency and its parent government department.

The Laboratory of the Government Chemist was one of the first group of Next Steps Agencies. In his foreword to the Laboratory's framework document of October 1989, Nicholas Ridley, Secretary of State for Trade and Industry, noted that the new Agency was to adopt an increasingly businesslike approach and would be expected to achieve 'demanding incremental improvements in overall efficiency and quality of service'. I was in no doubt that, having been appointed from outside the civil service, I was expected to accelerate this process.

The Laboratory's origins dated back to 1842 when The Laboratory of the Board of Excise was founded in the City of London by Mr George Phillips. At this time adulteration of tobacco, prohibited under the recent Pure Tobacco Act, was widespread. Phillips developed methods to detect a remarkable range of adulterants such as sugar, molasses, various leaves, chicory, rhubarb – the list was infinite – and he appeared in many court cases where traders were prosecuted for cheating the taxman. Work to protect Government revenue continued to be the main occupation until 1875 when the Laboratory, then housed in Somerset House, was appointed 'referee analyst' under the new Sale of Food and Drugs Act. This was an important piece of legislation specifically designed to protect the consumer rather than the revenue, by ensuring, for example, that milk had not been watered down. The role of the Government Chemist in ensuring the safety and quality of foods and consumer products continues to this day.

The decision to set up an official Government Laboratory under Dr (later Sir) Edward Thorpe was an important milestone and led to a move to purpose-built facilities in Clement's Inn Passage, off the Strand in London, in 1901. In 1911 the Government Laboratory was given independent status as the Department of the Government Chemist with the Principal, Sir James Dobbie FRS, and subsequent heads of the Laboratory given the title of 'Government Chemist'. When I was appointed chief executive in 1991, I was also appointed Government Chemist and I took on the responsibility, under legislation dating back to the nineteenth century, to act as a referee in disputes over analytical measurements likely to be used as evidence in civil courts.

In the period after the outbreak of the First World War, the Laboratory's scientific reputation grew and young chemists of higher academic attainment were recruited. On his appointment in 1921 Sir Robert Robinson FRS was asked to undertake investigations in areas of general interest to the public: the carriage of dangerous goods, atmospheric pollution, and the possible dangers to health arising from the use of lead tetraethyl in motor spirit. After a period of deep involvement in the war effort, the first decade after the Second World War was a period of evolutionary change and the Laboratory introduced new techniques, including X-ray diffraction and infrared spectrophotometry and embarked on new projects, including involvement in the Geological Survey. In 1959 the Laboratory lost its quasi-independence and was incorporated into the Department of Scientific and Industrial Research. In 1964 it moved to new 'temporary' premises south of the River Thames in Cornwall House, Waterloo.

Four major developments stand out from the 1980s. First, thanks to the foresight of Dr Ron Coleman, then Government Chemist, the Laboratory became involved in the industrial applications of biotechnology, managing a programme on behalf of the Department of Trade and Industry (DTI), by now the parent department in charge of the Laboratory of the Government Chemist. The Laboratory also took important steps to increase the strength of its own microbiological, and subsequently analytical molecular biological, effort.

Secondly, with important input from Alex Williams (Government Chemist from 1987 to 1991) a White Paper, '*Measuring up to the Competition*', identified the need for the National Measurement System to embrace chemical measurement. This led to the launch of the Valid Analytical Measurement (VAM) programme which continues today (as the Chemical and Biological Metrology programme) and has gained a high reputation internationally. Thirdly, the uncertainty over the future location of the Laboratory was removed with the decision to move from Cornwall House to new, purpose-built facilities at Teddington, adjacent to the National Physical Laboratory and Bushy Park. Finally, becoming an Agency within DTI set a direction for the organisation which could not be reversed.

When I arrived in 1991, I was struck by the contrasting aspects of the organisation that employed 345 people and cost £13 million a year to run. Many of the staff had worked at the Laboratory for a long time; they were proud of the past and were beginning to prepare to celebrate the 150th anniversary of the foundation of the Laboratory. The culture was very much rooted in the past and was inward-looking in that there was surprisingly little scientific exchange with other organisations in the UK and overseas. Longstanding work on, for example, the classification of import tariffs, where the Laboratory's technical word was virtually law, had led to a rather arrogant approach to public sector customers, who might have to wait months before the Laboratory ruled, for import duty purposes, on such arcane matters as when a biscuit was really a cake. Not untypical of the civil service at the time, when I first met staff they were frequently introduced by their grade before their name. As the new Government Chemist I was treated with respect (many surprised me by addressing me as 'Sir') but also a measure of suspicion as an outsider. However, by contrast, the Laboratory was housed in an impressive modern new laboratory, one of the leading facilities of its kind in Europe, and the organisation had blazed a trail in becoming one of the first Next Steps Agencies. There was an awareness that change was necessary, but little idea what form such change would take.

I soon discovered that there were some fundamental weaknesses in the organisation. I had inherited a 'corporate plan' (a requirement of all Next Steps Agencies) which rightly forecast increasing costs associated with being housed in the new building. However, in order to balance the books, and without any reference to markets or customers, the plan envisaged growth in receipts from unspecified sources. Just before I arrived there had been a re-organisation which created numerous new cost centres, but management information was dire and I felt that integration, rather than the fragmentation that had been introduced, was what was required. Moreover, although the organisation was housed in impressive facilities, some of the science was disappointing and there had been under-investment in new analytical techniques. In this context, however, an encouraging feature on the horizon was that my new colleague Roy Dietz, who with Ron Coleman had established DTI's Biotechnology Unit, had just set up a small unit for analytical molecular biology and had plans to set up a similar unit of just four scientists to undertake 'strategic research'.

My early days also involved learning what it was to be a senior civil servant. Having met the DTI permanent secretary, Sir Peter Gregson, shortly after arriving in the new job, I attended his monthly meetings of 'heads of management units' which gave me an insight into the workings of Government and the issues of the period leading up to the 1992 election when it appeared that the Conservative government under John Major was doomed. Witnessing how the civil servants in DTI prepared for a possible change in government was fascinating and, despite claims regarding the politicisation of the civil service, I was impressed by the professionalism and detached neutrality of my colleagues. Of course, DTI ministerial changes were, and unfortunately have continued to be, a very regular occurrence; the Secretary of State for Trade and Industry at the time, Peter Lilley, was the seventh since 1983. Whatever colour the new government, there was likely to be yet another change in the Secretary of State. It was hardly surprising, therefore, that my first impressions of the department were that it lacked direction and was happy to be distracted by issues surrounding the new Agencies and what should, or should not, be delegated to them.

During my first year I also met regularly with Ron Coleman, the Chief Engineer and Scientist, together with the heads of the other DTI laboratories (the National Physical Laboratory, the National Engineering Laboratory and Warren Spring Laboratory) when we discussed common issues. I learned that a High Level Mission to Japan on Analytical Instrumentation was on the agenda and I was expected to lead it. There was little time left to get it organised and, while DTI and Foreign Office officials did the spade work, making arrangements for visits to nearly 20 organisations, I rapidly become involved in identifying suitable representatives from industry to form the team of eight (plus officials) who would make up the Mission. The Mission took place in August/ September 1991 and aimed to investigate technical developments and future market opportunities for analytical instruments in Japan. The conclusions were sobering for the UK representatives; it was clear that Japanese industry was prepared to invest substantially for the longer term and, although the UK had a long history of analytical expertise, the Japanese were ahead in many aspects of the applications of new analytical technology. The observations the Mission made in relation to analytical science could have been made more generally in relation to the UK's strength in scientific research but weakness in its industrial and commercial exploitation. The culture in the UK has changed enormously over the last couple of decades, but I was certainly impressed by Japanese persistence during the development stage of innovation and the apparent willingness of their financial institutions to wait for long periods before achieving financial returns.

In getting to know both the Laboratory and the DTI I was very lucky to be helped by the Director of Resources, John Reynolds, a career civil servant who for my nearly five years as part of DTI was a kind and loyal lieutenant. John had worked in several departments, including a secondment to the Cabinet Office, and he knew his way around Whitehall. On many occasions he tactfully steered me out of trouble, and he helped guide the organisation through the difficult period leading up to privatisation. Within weeks of my arrival, it became apparent that we were not going to meet the ambitious budget that my predecessor had set and I set about looking for economies while John pulled strings with his contacts in Whitehall to winkle out additional funding. The problem was that we had to balance the trading accounts (broadly equivalent to a commercial profit and loss account) while at the same time staying within 'the Vote', the cash allocation which had been included in the budget approved by ministers. These two targets sometimes pulled in different directions, but I quickly learned that, while cash control during the year, unlike for a business, was not regarded as being of any consequence, achieving the 'Vote' or cash balance at the end of the year was the highest priority, in spite of the lip service paid to Agency trading accounts. In the event, the Laboratory met both targets and my first annual report (a glossy company-like annual report was a key feature of Next Steps Agencies) gave a reasonably upbeat message.

Another aspect of being chief executive of a Next Steps Agency was the requirement to answer Parliamentary Questions directly, rather than via a minister. Although ministers were accountable to Parliament and answered questions relating to policy, questions on operational matters could be directed to the relevant agency. The answers from agency chief executives were published in Hansard. I was initially rather naive about this process, and when asked a question about my overseas travel costs I provided a very full answer. I had not appreciated that the Member of Parliament asking the question had posed a similar question to all Next Steps Agencies chief executives, most of whom had provided a standard answer to the effect that the cost of obtaining such detailed information could not be justified. My answer stood out rather awkwardly among the others, and I quickly learned how civil servants handled such questions, never volunteering more information than was strictly necessary. (Public bodies are now required under Freedom of Information legislation to be more forthcoming with information.)

Agency status meant that all our work was carried out under 'contracts' with our government customers. These were not necessarily written agreements and did not always have financial limits, but the customer-contractor principle applied in one form or another to all the Laboratory's work. The largest programme was funded by the DTI under the National Measurement System and was aimed at helping industry achieve valid and comparable measurements. The impetus for this programme came from the move towards a single European market where compliance with regulation (say the amount of lead in toys) established in one European country had to be accepted by another. As mentioned above, in 1989 a White Paper, "*Measuring up to the Competition*" (CM 728) had set out the rationale for government funding of work on standards, including a system for chemical measurements, similar to the international system for weights and measures, to ensure traceability and comparability of measurements. The Valid Analytical Measurement (VAM) 'contract' rapidly became the backbone of the Laboratory of the Government Chemist's work and included work to develop so-called reference materials – the chemical equivalent of physical standards – and develop authoritative analytical methods. The programme also included work to increase awareness of the need for comparable measurements amongst the analytical community, which brought with it the very positive requirement to interact with other organisations much more widely than in the past. So with my Government Chemist hat on, I had a new role to promote the importance of valid analytical measurements and this took me to many different conferences and gatherings of laboratory managers and industrialists. It also provided me with an excellent reason to invite senior people from industry, other parts of government and academia to visit our impressive facility at Teddington and to promote the role and work of the Laboratory. I ensured that these visits were carefully planned and choreographed to make sure that visitors left with a positive impression of our staff and of the dynamism of a changing organisation. Some of the early visitors included Sir Brian Unwin, Chairman of HM Customs and Excise (an important customer of the Laboratory), Dr Peter Bunyan, Chief Scientist at the Ministry of Agriculture, Fisheries and Food (again an important customer), and Sir Peter Kemp, the permanent secretary at the Cabinet Office who had pioneered the Next Steps programme.

Another visitor during 1991 was Lord Reay, the Minister for Industry and Technology, whom I had been called to see shortly after my appointment. It had been my first meeting with a minister in my new role and I was told in advance that he was to chair a meeting in Brussels on biotechnology and wanted some background information. To be certain that I could answer any technical questions, I took with me my colleague Roy Dietz who had a deep understanding of the subject and of the emerging UK biotechnology industry. Lord Reay's first question to me was: "What exactly is biotechnology?" My initial reaction was: Is he joking? However, I quickly realised that the minister was serious and had very little understanding of science in general or biotechnology in particular. He was visibly relieved when I began my reply by drawing on illustrations from wine and cheese making. However, the division bell sounded and he was whisked away by a minder to vote in a division in the House of Lords, so that Roy and I were able to prepare a fuller answer before he returned half an hour later. I never found out how his meeting in Brussels went.

The celebrations in 1992 which we planned to mark the 150th anniversary of the foundation of the Laboratory provided an excellent opportunity for promoting the organisation. Relations between the Laboratory of the Government Chemist and The Royal Society of Chemistry (RSC) had not in the recent past been good. My predecessor was a physicist rather than a chemist, and RSC, in particular its Analytical Division, had reacted in a petty and narrow-minded way to his appointment. Shortly after my appointment I was made a Fellow of the RSC and I had been invited to various functions. The anniversary celebrations provided the opportunity to complete the rapprochement and to develop a more cordial relationship with the Society (which was to be very important later). We jointly organised an international conference on analytical science which was held at the University of Reading in September that year. The conference, which was attended by 400 delegates, was opened by Geoff Robinson, who had succeeded Ron Coleman (who had retired at the time of the election) as Chief Engineer and Scientist, and I gave an address highlighting the history of the Laboratory and its relationship with the Society of Analytical Chemists, the forerunner of RSC's Analytical Division. A number of open days were held at Teddington, including a social day for families and friends, and the year's festivities ended with a formal dinner at the Apothecaries' Hall, which we chose as the venue to reflect the long history of the Laboratory. Senior representatives of government, industry and the academic world attended a convivial event, at which Sir Brian Unwin proposed the toast to the Laboratory and Edward Leigh MP, the new Undersecretary of State for Industry, replied. To coincide with the anniversary we published a history of the laboratory, '*Weighed in the Balance*', which had been started by one of my predecessors as Government Chemist, Harold Egan, and was completed by our librarian, Peter Hammond.

Although the accounting system was arcane, there were some advantages to the Agency being within the civil service. It transpired that there was a budget in DTI associated with capital building works and John Reynolds and I successfully bid for a scheme to modernise two run-down Victorian houses on the Teddington site next to the laboratory. One was converted into offices and a small social club and the other into a crèche for children of employees from the three DTI laboratories on the Teddington site. John and I were particularly committed to providing a children's nursery since many of our staff had difficulty making arrangements for suitable childcare. A competition among staff to name the nursery came up with the name 'Bushy Tails' (because the site was adjacent to Bushy Park and a squirrel motif was thought attractive) and the management of the nursery was contracted out. We invited Sir Brian Unwin (head of one of our major customers, HM Customs & Excise and chairman of the Civil Service Sports Council) to open the social club and DTI's permanent secretary, Sir Peter Gregson, to open the crèche, and we used publicity arising from the opening of these facilities to promote the Laboratory as a progressive employer. Bushy Tails was an immediate success and proved to be invaluable in helping us recruit and retain excellent young staff. Over subsequent years, I received much positive feedback on how staff and their children had valued Bushy Tails; it certainly contributed to the new culture I wanted to create in the organisation.

The unexpected Conservative victory in April 1992 led to yet another change of Secretary of State, but the new incoming minister, Michael Heseltine, chose to be called by the historic title 'President of the Board of Trade' to reflect what he planned to be a change of focus for the Department of Trade and Industry. Heseltine's arrival sent a wave through the Department. The DTI had been a ragbag of regulatory and industry support divisions and had not long before absorbed the Department of Energy, and the immediate period following the election was taken up with a major reorganisation to create industry-facing divisions with clear objectives and financial targets. Heseltine introduced his MINIS system (Management Information System for Ministers) which he had adopted when he was at the Department of the Environment. For an Agency such as ours it was rather old hat, but it certainly focused minds in other parts of the DTI. However, one consequence of the reorganisation was that the Laboratory lost the Biotechnology Unit which was moved from Teddington to Whitehall to the newly created Chemicals and Biotechnology Division. Rather to my surprise, Roy Dietz, who as head of the Unit had done much to develop its, and hence the Laboratory's, reputation throughout the burgeoning UK biotechnology industry, decided not to transfer to DTI headquarters but to remain as a director of the Laboratory of the Government Chemist. Nevertheless, the loss of the Unit was a blow, not only because of its prestige but also because it made a much-needed contribution to offsetting the Laboratory's heavy overheads.

However, there were other changes in the offing. The new government was introducing targets for 'market testing', where a part of each department's work had to be considered for contracting out. There was considerable resistance to this throughout Whitehall, and DTI mandarins asked that we should provide data to show how much of what we did was already contracted out and to give evidence of money saved, or not, as the case might be. It was impressive to see the civil service responding to a threat!

There were certainly aspects of the 'market testing' policy which were inconsistent. Agencies had been created to apply new methods of management to executive functions – from Highways to Child Support. Were they now expected to market test their work? If so, fundamental questions needed to be addressed: should the whole function of the agency be 'contracted out' or privatised? During my first meeting with the new Undersecretary of State for Industry, Edward Leigh, after the election, he made clear his own view that privatisation of the DTI's laboratories should be on the agenda, but he did little to move this forward; I suspected he thought there was more mileage in looking at the Post Office, for which he was also responsible.

As the first of the DTI laboratories to become an Agency, the Laboratory of the Government Chemist was already embarking on the three-year review of the Agency's framework document, required under the Next Steps Agency 'rules', and DTI economists were busy trying to evaluate the cost/benefits of the Laboratory's status. With so many external developments and a huge number of internal management issues to consider, I decided to take the 14 senior managers of the Laboratory for a two-day intensive meeting in June, away from our Teddington site, to review progress on changes which had been initiated – new approaches to customers, new pricing structures, new finance and IT systems, benchmarking of key indicators – and to set a new mission and clear objectives for the organisation. I wanted to galvanise the management team for the many challenges on the horizon.

The management meeting partly served its purpose; the mission statement and objectives which were developed, and issued later, provided a basis for the new corporate plan which was required for the Agency, and they were a useful focus during the coming difficult four years. However, the meeting also revealed the commercial weakness of the organisation. Our senior managers had risen through the ranks of the scientific civil service, and although they recognised that change was coming, they displayed a feeling of helplessness in coping with what they saw to be external threats. Moreover, among the group were some who would never survive in the private sector.

However, there were other aspects of the management of the Agency which were not straightforward. The Laboratory management was overseen by a steering board which was chaired by the senior civil servant in charge of the 'division' and included civil servants from DTI and from the Laboratory's customer departments. There were a couple of 'external' members who were there to provide a more commercial perspective. When I joined in 1991 the steering board chairman was Ron Coleman, who had previously managed the Laboratory in the years leading up to its move to Teddington and the change to Agency status. Ron understood science and had been a manager. He was supportive of the changes I wanted to make and gave me some useful advice on how to get things done within the government machine. When he retired, his job was split. A new chief engineer and scientist, Dr Geoff Robinson, was appointed from outside the civil service (he'd been at IBM) and the 'ownership' function for the DTI laboratories was put into a new division headed by Tony Lane. Tony, an Oxford PPE graduate who had spent most of his civil service career in policy departments, took over the chairmanship of our steering board. Tony seemed to me to exemplify the mandarin class of civil servant. He was charming and interesting but clearly more preoccupied with policy than with what he regarded as the mundane task of delivering services. Quarterly steering board meetings were very long and took the form of debates, with each side of the argument being fully evaluated (by Tony); the conclusions and actions seemed to be regarded as secondary. However, Tony supported me in arranging some changes to the 'external' membership of the steering board; John Cox, director-general of the Chemical Industries Association and Paul Winson, formerly a marketing director of Oxford Instruments, joined the board and provided a more commercial perspective which put us in a stronger position for the choppy waters ahead.

As 1992 progressed, in spite of the positive spirit generated by our anniversary celebrations and the reputation we were gaining as a well-run Agency, my private doubts over whether the Laboratory could ever be viable as an independent entity increased. The problem was simple. In the past the organisation had specified the fees to be charged to government customers. Now, customers were rightly challenging our high fees and were questioning whether the work was really necessary or could be done elsewhere. We were housed in a wonderful new laboratory, but the rent and rates were expected to increase sharply and utility costs were enormous. Our utilisation of space, whatever the scientists who had helped design the building thought, was very poor. The fact that we were able to expand our income slightly in 1992/3 and record a small surplus was a real achievement, but was it sustainable?

It seemed to me that one obvious way forward would be to seek to merge with another organisation so that the high 'fixed' costs associated with our prestigious facility would be shared over a larger business. In looking at potential candidates for merger within the public sector, I hoped that a White Paper initiated by William Waldegrave, who had become Chancellor of the Duchy of Lancaster (and Minister for Science) after the 1992 election, might provide me with an opportunity. The Cabinet Office White Paper promised a systematic examination of all Government science and technology Agencies. Surely some rationalisation and mergers would follow?

Partly to discuss such developments and partly to exchange experiences of managing technical agencies, the Government Research Agencies chief executives (neatly referred to as GRACE) started to meet every few months. It was a rather heterogeneous group which included experienced businessmen such as John Chisholm, who ran DERA (much later to be privatised as Qinetic) and Bill Edgar, who ran the National Engineering Laboratory (sold into the private sector in 1995) as well as practised civil servants such as Peter Stanley, who ran MAFF's Central Science Laboratory, Peter Clapham, director of the National Physical Laboratory, and Roger Courtenay who ran the Building Research Establishment. There were also rather more academic figures such as Julian Hunt FRS, who ran the Met Office, and Anthony Beattie, a development economist in charge of the National Resources Institute (later to merge with the University of Greenwich).

While they provided a useful discussion forum, GRACE meetings confirmed how difficult it was to get agreements between Agencies and their parent department, let alone any agreement between government departments. I was therefore not hopeful that a strategic rationalisation of government laboratories and facilities would emerge from the Cabinet Office review. I did not think LGC had time to await the results of reviews and decided to draw up a list of possible targets for us to approach directly, taking into account scientific synergies as well as geography.

My first initiative was to try to intervene in the planning process for the relocation of MAFF's Central Science Laboratory (CSL) from Slough and other disparate sites to a major new laboratory at York. The logic of my argument was that if some parts of CSL's work were transferred to Teddington, savings could be made by building a smaller facility at York.

Chapter 1 The Agency years

I put my proposal in a confidential letter to Peter Bunyan, MAFF's chief scientist. The initiative was unwelcome. A business case had already been made, and agreed by the Treasury, for the construction of a major new facility at York on the basis of savings in closing several small and, no doubt, inefficient MAFF facilities. My proposal would have involved an inter-departmental assessment. Peter politely acknowledged my proposal but I never received a proper response. In the event, the York laboratory was later to prove something of a white elephant, confirming the views I had expressed to MAFF.

My second initiative was aimed at the Home Office which was in the process of reviewing the future management arrangements for the Metropolitan Police Forensic Science Laboratory (MPFSL), housed in a rather old police building in Lambeth. I went to see Ian Burns, the civil servant in charge of the police department at the Home Office and set out the savings that might be made if the MPFSL were to move to Teddington and be merged with LGC. This meeting precipitated a visit from Graham Angel, the 'Receiver' of the Metropolitan Police (a strange title for the head of administration responsible for the Met's enormous budget). My merger plan had certainly set the cat among the pigeons and it was many months before I received any response to my proposals. It transpired that ministerial exchanges between Michael Heseltine and Michael Howard (the Home Secretary) followed, but the idea was adroitly kicked into touch by the mandarins. Eventually, the Home Office reverted to its own plan which was to merge the MPFSL with the Home Office Forensic Science Service. As Michael Heseltine had warned me, it was extremely difficult to pull off a change like this across government departments.

Another option for merger was more complicated. Warren Spring Laboratory in Stevenage, which was also a DTI Agency and was engaged in environmental research and development, from recycling to marine pollution, was housed in outdated facilities at Stevenage. It had developed a plan to sell its site to Glaxo and, with the £30 million or so proceeds, move to new facilities nearby. Apparently, this proposal was announced without the prior knowledge of DTI's President. When he was told of the plan he decided to appoint outside consultants, PA Consulting Group, to review whether it represented 'best value' of available options. With Peter Clapham, Director of the National Physical Laboratory, which was on the same site as the Laboratory of the Government Chemist at Teddington, I proposed that Warren Spring could be moved to Teddington, thus creating a single DTI research centre and increasing the utilisation of the site, especially LGC's building. To my disappointment, PA recommended moving Warren Spring to AEA Technology at Harwell (which was subsequently privatised). In the event, Warren Spring was effectively closed; only part of the work was transferred to Harwell and that subsequently fared badly as a consequence of the disastrous mismanagement of the privatised AEA Technology.

When Michael Heseltine visited the Laboratory of the Government Chemist on 26 April 1993 it was already clear that he wanted to privatise all the DTI laboratories. I explained some of the difficulties that might arise in trying to create a truly commercial business from an organisation with a modest income which used very expensive assets. The legal position of the Government Chemist as a referee analyst was complicated and would need to be resolved. Perhaps an independent, non-profit-distributing structure was the most appropriate? His visit around the Teddington laboratory went well and at the end we had a short but useful discussion which was interrupted by a phone call from the Chancellor of the Exchequer, Mr Lamont. I was impressed how Mr Heseltine could switch from the relatively minor matter of the future of the Laboratory of the Government Chemist to major issues surrounding the UK economy and back again. After dealing with so many people in government who had little understanding of running a business, it was refreshing to talk to a senior minister who instinctively grasped the issues.

Shortly after his visit, Michael Heseltine announced a review of the status of all the DTI laboratories and the consultants KPMG were appointed in June 1993 with a remit to examine options for privatisation and closure. Heseltine was pre-empting the recommendation of the White Paper on Science and Technology, published in May, which proposed a government-wide review of science and technology agencies. For the next two and a half years, the status of LGC was in limbo and a great deal of my time was involved in the privatisation process. However, the running of the Agency had to go on and, in some ways, the uncertainty hanging over the organisation facilitated some major changes which might have been more difficult to achieve in more stable times.

Chapter 1 The Agency years

Central to the Laboratory's mission was its responsibility for fostering quality in analytical and molecular biological measurement, and ensuring the quality of services provided to customers had never been more important. The approach to quality had several strands which included the use of quality systems – documents, procedures, and instructions for all critical tasks. The Laboratory of the Government Chemist had pioneered the use of laboratory accreditation and had advised many other organisations on how this could be achieved. Not long after my arrival, we decided to go further and seek certification of all our activities – laboratory and administrative – under BS 5750 Part 1 (ISO 9001). In 1994 we successfully passed an assessment by quality assessors from the British Standards Institution which led to registration; at around the same time we were registered as compliant to Good Laboratory Practice (GLP). All this helped promote the Laboratory's pre-eminent position as a centre of excellence in analytical science at a time when the financial position of the organisation was becoming less secure.

The Agency desperately needed to change its personnel management procedures and now had some freedom to break with civil service practice. With the appointment of a new head of human resources from outside the civil service, we were able to press ahead with introducing 'performance management' and a modest bonus scheme, which we had to agree with the Treasury. Although we were a scientific organisation, we were miles behind in the use of information technology. We needed to develop a strategy for office and laboratory systems, install the necessary local area network (LAN), and train staff in the use of computer systems. Following a review, commissioned by the Ministry of Defence, of the procurement of food for the armed services, the future viability of a small outstation laboratory at Gosport which undertook food quality assurance specifically for the MoD was in doubt. In May 1994 I announced our intention to close this unit and to transfer the reduced amount of work to Teddington.

More fundamental was my decision, despite the uncertainty surrounding the future status of the agency, to undertake a far-reaching 'operational review' using a technique – activity value analysis – which I had adopted in a previous job when I was asked to reduce overheads expenditure by 20%. I hoped that such a review of the agency would be equally successful in weeding out waste and reducing the cost base and we appointed Coopers & Lybrand to help. The objectives of the review were to identify key areas for improvement in productivity by examining the processes for generating business, meeting customer needs, and supporting the Laboratory's operations. The review began with a high-level analysis of the business, some customer interviews, and a pilot staff survey; this was followed by an in-depth examination of almost all working processes. The review involved a high degree of staff participation and included all departments.

The operational review took several months to complete and was brought to a head in November 1994 when the senior management had to decide on where and how changes should be made. There were some far-reaching decisions to be made, some of which – creating an organisation with fewer layers and shorter lines of communication – would be difficult to achieve within a structure which was still determined by civil service grades. However, the senior team agreed on some fundamental changes to the organisation, management structure and business processes. An implementation plan was agreed, with a timetable to ensure all changes were made by April 1995, the beginning of the next financial year. With major savings in fixed costs in mind, the review led to the clearance of two laboratory blocks, about a quarter of the laboratory space at Teddington. A new organisation focused on market sectors was introduced and some fundamental changes were made to support areas. Over the period of the review and beyond, staff numbers were reduced by over 25% by natural wastage and a programme of early retirement/ voluntary redundancy.

In managing major change, communication is essential. It was vital to ensure that staff understood the reason for, and the objectives of, the changes and were aware of how they would be achieved. The survival of the organisation depended on radical productivity improvements which would be difficult for many to accept. I spent a great deal of time in discussions with small groups, giving regular presentations to all staff, writing pieces in our staff newsletter, and talking to people in the workplace. I held many meetings with longer-serving staff, who had worked loyally for the organisation over many years but who now found change on this scale too difficult to accept. The early retirement schemes enabled some of them to leave with dignity and to pursue other interests. In hindsight, I was perhaps optimistic about being able to change attitudes among a small minority of diehards; I went to huge lengths and wasted time trying to address their concerns and should have been tougher with those who did not want to leave and remained as obstacles to change. The operational changes also affected our customers. I visited many of them, and key government stakeholders, and invited them to Teddington. My programme of VIP visits, which included some senior industrialists and eminent scientists, aimed to ensure maximum awareness of the positive changes taking place in the Laboratory. Some of the visits also served to 'educate' politicians on the challenges of managing scientific organisations. For example, during a visit by the 13th Earl Ferrers, PC, then Minister of State at the Home Office, we discussed the subject of pay for scientists in the civil service. I told him the salary of a scientist who had a PhD and several years' research experience whom he had met during an excellent laboratory presentation. He was visibly shocked at how little she received, commenting that his cook was paid more. Lord Ferrers was clearly impressed by what he saw on his visit; as he left he said that you could always tell whether chickens were happy by putting your head inside the chicken house, and that during his visit he had gained the impression of a contented group of people. I took this observation as a compliment!

Crucial to the future of the Laboratory, whatever form that might take, was a greater focus on marketing and business development. I had recruited a new head of marketing shortly after my appointment; the appointment had cause a stir since he was in a senior post but only in his early thirties. He was frustrated by the entrenched conservatism of some of the older managers and, understandably, moved on after a couple of years. We advertised the post, which led to one of the best appointments I have ever made. Dr Ray Ah-Sun had recently decided to take early retirement from Shell rather than be transferred to a post in the US with the sale of a specialist chemicals business where he had a senior post in business development. He had an interesting background – childhood in Mauritius but higher education in England. English was his third language after Chinese and French. I interviewed him several times before I could fathom him. Between interviews he wrote a lucid account of what the Laboratory of the Government Chemist required and what he would offer. I was frankly surprised that such an experienced manager would want to join an organisation in such a state of flux, but he was clearly enthusiastic about my approach to management and business. Ray's contribution in business development over the next ten years and more was a key factor in LGC's future success.

For the staff, the internal and operational changes within the organisation and the new emphasis on markets and customers, and the many other changes, served to distract attention from the mounting uncertainty over the future of the Agency. However, once the President had announced a review of future options for the Laboratory in 1993, the dominant item on the agenda for the Agency, as far as DTI was concerned, was privatisation.

Chapter 2: *My management buy-out*

*Reviews of Next Steps Agencies – Alternative forms of privatisation –
The Laboratory of the Government Chemist up for sale –
My decision to bid – 3i and The Royal Society of Chemistry –
Negotiations with DTI – Forming a new company*

The review that Michael Heseltine commissioned from the consultants KPMG of the DTI research agencies – the National Physical Laboratory, the National Engineering Laboratory, and the Laboratory of the Government Chemist – got under way in June 1993 and was a major undertaking. The scope of KPMG's study was wide: to examine the role, activities and business performance of each of the laboratories; to assess and make recommendations on the feasibility, advantages and disadvantages of changes in the ownership of the laboratories; and, in the event of a recommendation to privatise, to submit advice on the range and feasibility of different types of buyers. The consultants were to consider the future for DTI as the owner of the laboratories, not as a customer, so they did not examine in detail the merits of the various science and technology programmes in the laboratories. The review was carried out by quite a large team at KPMG under the leadership of Chris Nicholson; the consultant appointed to look at the Laboratory of the Government Chemist was Rob Wylie, who had previously worked for Shell and who was later to found WHEB, a successful investment company specialising in environmental projects.

I felt it was important that LGC should not remain passive; rather, we should formulate our own proposals to put to the consultants. I also urged the 'external' members of our steering board to arrange to see the consultants, who would no doubt already have been fully briefed about LGC by Tony Lane and his DTI colleagues. The gist of the proposals that LGC management submitted in July was that privatisation was a feasible option, but that major changes would be necessary before this could be achieved. Any owner would need to be able to demonstrate impartiality and independence if the organisation was to continue to fulfil the legislative requirements of the Government Chemist as a referee analyst. The Laboratory's work for HM Customs and Excise and MAFF often required our staff to appear as expert witnesses in the courts, where impartiality and independence were crucial.

We suggested that the form of privatisation which could probably best meet these requirements was a company limited by guarantee (CLG), a non-profit-distributing company. A number of research associations had become CLGs, including the Hydraulics Research Institute which Michael Heseltine had privatised during his time as Environment Minister. I visited several such organisations, including the Electrical Research Association (ELA) and the Scientific Instruments Research Association (SIRA), to learn about the pros and cons of CLGs, and the consultants at KPMG did their homework on such structures.

The review took a long time, partly because of Michael Heseltine's illness during his visit to Venice in June and his absence during the summer months. Still finding civil service procedures rather baffling, I was surprised how even relatively minor matters were delayed because of the absence of the Secretary of State. However, from my point of view, the delay in agreement of LGC's corporate plan was not simply a minor glitch. All agencies were required to have corporate plans, which were effectively the contract between the chief executive and the minister which set out how the agency should be run over a three-year period. Although the delay was understandable, the absence of an agreed plan made it difficult to take any management decisions. Eventually, the then junior minister, Patrick McLoughlin MP, who had visited LGC during the summer (it was always easier to arrange ministerial visits during the parliamentary recess) was persuaded in the autumn to approve a plan which would allow us at least to continue to operate and to embark on a restructuring initiative to achieve cost reductions. However, in many respects our plan had already been overtaken by events. The tight expenditure settlements across Whitehall would inevitably lead to a reduction in customer support and, in view of the uncertainty over the future of the Laboratory, work on a new Framework Document, which had started nearly two years earlier, seemed rather pointless. All attention was now focused on the KPMG review.

The KPMG team consulted widely and, in particular, sought views on ownership options from our main customers. The internal DTI customers were far from keen on privatisation, but felt unable to express views which went against ministerial policy. HMCE and MAFF officials were positively hostile to the idea. After the production of business plans and a full analysis of the options for all three DTI laboratories, a draft report was available for discussion at a meeting with the President and his advisers on 15th December. The meeting also considered a study (by property consultants Puller Peiser) about the rationalisation of the Teddington site, home to the Laboratory of the Government Chemist, the National Physical Laboratory and the National Weights and Measures Laboratory, as well as the beautiful 18th century Bushy House, which housed some of NPL's laboratories. The possible development of the Teddington site, involving residential and retail options, was a major part of the discussion and during the meeting seemed, incredibly, to be given greater attention than the future of three renowned national institutions.

However, the broad framework that KPMG proposed for the future of the three laboratories was accepted. For LGC, three options were put forward: status quo, privatisation as a non-profit-distributing company, and closure. It was clear that closure would be tricky (and expensive) and that the status quo was not a likely outcome. A company limited by guarantee was likely to satisfy the requirements for independence and impartiality. The option for NEL was likely to be a trade sale and for NPL a publicly-owned but contractor-operated company.

During the weeks that followed, detailed proposals for the three laboratories were formulated, and discussions took place with the Treasury. Bill Edgar, chief executive of NEL, and I were broadly content with the direction events were taking, although I always stressed the need for restructuring to enable LGC to be viable. Peter Clapham, NPL's chief executive, was less happy at the prospect of a major national measurement institute being run by a private company, and the Teddington site, where NPL was housed in old buildings, remained a key issue to sort out.

At the end of March (1994) Michael Heseltine agreed to meet representatives of the steering boards of the three laboratories. Arriving late for the meeting, he simply asked who wanted to speak first. A member of the NPL steering board expressed great concern at the prospect of privatisation, but it was fascinating to see how an experienced politician shot down the arguments one by one. I had rehearsed with John Cox and Paul Winson, members of the Laboratory's steering board, the key points they would make, and John presented an excellent account of issues affecting the Laboratory of the Government Chemist. Although there were undoubtedly some difficult issues surrounding the privatisation of the Laboratory, we made clear that we wanted it to be achieved successfully and I was encouraged by the degree of engagement at the top of DTI.

On 14 April Michael Heseltine issued a statement on plans for the future of DTI's laboratories. He said that although the laboratories had made impressive progress as Executive Agencies, he was convinced that they would respond best to the challenges they faced if they were to move to the private sector where they would be 'set free from the constraints of operating within government'. Referring to LGC, Heseltine said:

> 'I have decided to pursue the recommendation of my consultants that it should be established as an independent non-profit-distributing company in the private sector. Preparations for this will be put in hand immediately, including a major restructuring programme, and I hope to complete the process by the end of 1995/96. However, my mind is not closed to the possibility of a trade sale of the LGC, if a suitable buyer comes forward who can demonstrate the requisite independence.'

After months of uncertainty, I was pleased with the outcome and in my letters to staff, customers and members of our steering board, and at a meeting with all staff the following day, I was upbeat in conveying the news that LGC was likely to become a non-profit-distributing company. Privately, I was particularly pleased that my restructuring programme (the 'operational review') would be supported and there would be finance available for early retirement and redundancy terms should this be necessary.

Shortly before the announcement, DTI had run a very rapid tender exercise to appoint a fresh set of consultants to help manage the privatisation process for each of the laboratories, and PA Consulting Group was appointed. PA got to work immediately, but found that, in LGC's case, it was not entirely straightforward. DTI officials were anxious about how they were to satisfy ministers that the rider about a 'suitable buyer' coming forward had been addressed. How were they to establish whether a suitable buyer who could 'demonstrate the requisite independence' existed? Indeed, what exactly was the 'requisite independence'?

During the next few months, progress was made in assembling data for an information memorandum and with the preparation of a model business plan for a company limited by guarantee, and I was also occupied in closing the Gosport outstation laboratory, completing the new quality system, and presenting LGC to a stream of visitors, including Sir Peter Gregson, DTI's permanent secretary, who visited the site for the first time, and Ian Johnson, then Assistant Commissioner of the Metropolitan Police who was curious about my proposal for a merger with the Metropolitan Police Forensic Science Laboratory. However, there was a feeling that no-one was really driving the privatisation process. It did not come as a surprise when it was announced that Tony Lane, the Assistant Secretary in charge of the DTI Laboratories, would be retiring early and would be replaced by Brian Hilton, who had been in the Prime Minister's Office in charge of the Citizen's Charter initiative and who had a reputation for getting things done.

Brian Hilton's arrival changed the atmosphere immediately. He was certainly different from other mandarins. Tall and with a beard, he came across rather as a sea captain, or even as an admiral! He had joined the civil service as a school leaver and had worked his way up from the bottom. He didn't display the rather embittered cynicism of some senior civil servants; rather, he was respectful of politicians and saw it as the civil servant's job to use his or her best efforts to implement policy. The course for the privatisation of DTI's laboratories had been set by ministers and Brian saw it as his job to steer the ship home in the shortest time possible. At a meeting with me and the external board members early in September, he set out a clear agenda for the programme. A privatisation team was set up with civil servants assigned to LGC. They produced charts showing the critical path and key decision points (GANTT charts) and also sent a letter to all staff with 'Guidance on conduct' during the privatisation process.

A survey was commissioned from Ove Arup & Partners and valuations were commissioned from Knight, Frank & Rutley of the Teddington buildings and surrounding land, and Grimley International Property Advisers of all the Laboratory's assets. A special survey of the 'Broderick Roofing' of the Teddington building, which had shown signs of blistering, had been carried out early in the year by Sandberg Consulting Engineers, and the environmental team of the Laboratory of the Government Chemist itself had been commissioned to carry out a full environmental site investigation. By the end of 1994 all the necessary information had been assembled and an information memorandum had been produced by DTI and PA Consulting Group (with a lot of help from LGC staff) which set out the background to privatisation and the objectives of the sale and a full description of the business, customers and resources of the Agency.

Brian Hilton's proposal for establishing whether a trade sale would be possible was simple; an advertisement would be put in the Financial Times inviting expressions of interest. So, in November 1994 the following advertisement appeared in the FT:

"The Laboratory of the Government Chemist: Private Ownership

The Department of Trade and Industry intends to transfer the Laboratory of the Government Chemist to private ownership by April 1996 either by a non-profit-distributing company or through a commercial sale of the business....

Organisations interested in purchasing the Laboratory as a business should write to Bob Collier at the DTI no later than 9th December 1994 setting out their initial qualifications and the rationale for their interest...."

At the January 1995 meeting of the Laboratory of the Government Chemist's steering board, Brian Hilton reported that there had been 40 responses to the advertisement in the Financial Times and that formal expressions of interest had subsequently been received from eight of these. A short list of five organisations had been selected and had been sent the bulky information memorandum (which had been completed in December).

One by one the short listed organisations visited the Laboratory. I was required to give a presentation and show them round, but Brian Hilton and his team were present to ensure proper conduct. Of those who visited, the most credible bidders were two water companies and a university. The recently privatised water utilities were desperately looking to diversify their businesses away from activities which were under the direct scrutiny of the regulator, Ofwat. They ran laboratories to ensure water quality and saw the opportunity to increase this non-regulated part of their business by expanding in the scientific services market.

The legal and financial arrangements for setting up a Company Limited by Guarantee (CLG) were pursued in parallel and the privatisation team was also working hard on the privatisation of the other two laboratories – the National Physical Laboratory and the National Engineering Laboratory. NEL was privatised through a trade sale in June 1995 (it ultimately became part of the TÜV SÜD Group) and a contract for running NPL was awarded to Serco in October 1995. LGC's privatisation was proving more difficult. The legal position of the Government Chemist, who was cited as referee analyst in several Acts of Parliament, made it difficult to envisage a straight sale of the organisation, if the Government Chemist was to remain part of it. However, if the Government Chemist were to be separate from the Laboratory, how would he or she be able to fulfil the statutory duties? DTI's lawyers examined every detail of the relevant legislation looking for a way forward. In the end, the situation was resolved by a scheme which involved the public appointment of the Government Chemist being made by DTI and a contract to carry out the function of the Government Chemist being awarded to the new private owner. However, all this was taking time, and there were delays in receiving proper bids from the short-listed organisations.

Against this background, running LGC was, understandably, becoming increasingly difficult. Early in 1995 we received news that we had lost a significant contract with the Intervention Board for analytical support on the determination of tariff classification. This work had been done by LGC for years but had been put out to tender partly as a result of the impending privatisation. In our bid we had reduced our prices considerably, but import tariffs were being lowered and the technical answer to such esoteric questions as to what makes basmati rice different from other rice – we were experts on this! – were of less significance than they had been in the past. So the technical part of the work was much reduced. However, losing the contract was a financial blow and it certainly did not help with the task of maintaining staff morale during a very uncertain period.

By April 1995 indicative proposals had been received by DTI for the purchase of the Laboratory and they decided to pursue two of them, together with the Company Limited by Guarantee option. Accompanied by Bob Collier, one of the DTI officials assigned to manage the privatisation, I visited the two potential trade buyers but was disappointed at their lack of vision for the future of the Laboratory were it to be part of their organisations. In the meantime my colleagues and I had our work cut out keeping the organisation together as well as working towards a new pay and grading system (project Prime) which would allow more sensible staff management arrangements.

Throughout this period I had been thinking hard about all the privatisation options. The CLG option now appeared less attractive. Although it satisfied many of the requirements for independence, there would be drawbacks in terms of the commercial and financial freedoms to develop in new directions. A trade buyer was certainly more likely to provide the financial support needed for an organisation which was still far from being self-sufficient commercially; moreover, such a new owner with an existing business could perhaps secure a future with more potential. As time passed, with no clear outcome in sight to the trade sale process, I began to conceive how I might myself create a company which would itself submit a bid.

I had enjoyed my time running the Laboratory of the Government Chemist Executive Agency and had developed respect for my scientific colleagues within the Agency, although there were very few people with any real experience of business. It had been hard building business within the civil service but the Laboratory would certainly have a much greater chance to develop outside government, free from the constraints of the civil service. As it stood, the organisation was barely viable as an independent entity; the substantial fixed costs were difficult to cover with business in danger of shrinking. Nevertheless, the possibility of taking full control of the organisation myself, and developing it in a direction that I would choose, was immensely appealing. It would present a wonderful opportunity to create my own company, pursuing business and scientific ideas and adopting values that I believed in.

Before I joined the Laboratory of the Government Chemist I had had some contact with private equity investors including 3i plc, a company which had been formed to invest in British companies as part of the post-war recovery. Some time before DTI launched the sale process, Matthew Young, a consultant to 3i with a particular interest in privatisations, had been to see me and, with DTI's agreement, I had been to meet a small team at 3i. These discussions had not gone further; it was far from clear at that stage how a management buy-out might work. However, as time passed I continued to think about possible ways in which a management buy-out could be made to work. A key moment for me was the publication of the annual report of the Royal Society of Chemistry (RSC). As a Fellow of the Society I was sent a copy, and it arrived through the post one Saturday morning. As I idly flicked through the pages, I came to the financial statements and noted that the Society had very substantial reserves (of the order of £30 million, as I recall). I already knew that the RSC, which had been represented on the High Level Mission to Japan I had led in 1991, was concerned about the UK's declining position in analytical science. Moreover, the Society had expressed concern about the damage that might result from the privatisation of the Laboratory of the Government Chemist. Would it be possible for this learned body, housed in Burlington House, to invest from their reserves in a company which I would form with the backing of 3i, and part of whose remit would be to become a vehicle for promoting RSC's interest in analytical science? The more I thought about it, the more it appeared that this creative idea could satisfy all the requirements of DTI, our customers and our staff. Was this the moment to launch a management buy-out bid, backed by RSC and 3i and to create a company which I would lead?

My first move was to have a long discussion with my wife, Jacqueline. Our happy life together had been shattered when our eldest daughter, Helen, had been suddenly taken ill with a brain tumour in 1978 when she was nearly three. Following an operation, Helen had been left totally disabled, unable to talk, feed herself or move her limbs. Jacquie and I looked after Helen and her two younger sisters, Catherine and Isobel, at our home in Abingdon, but Helen's serious condition, and the uncertainty over her future, placed heavy restrictions on our life. Looking back, it amazes me how Jacquie managed to look after our young family, helped found the first children's hospice, Helen House, named after our daughter, wrote a book on the foundation of Helen House and the philosophy of children's hospice care, chaired a BBC advisory committee, and was a job-share lecturer at Oxford College of Further Education. Our lives were full and, despite the constant undertow of deep sadness and the exhaustion of caring for Helen, happy.

Jacquie was of course aware of the uncertainty hanging over LGC and that my contract running the Laboratory was due to end in a year's time. I explained that, if I were to form a company to bid to acquire LGC, I would have to invest my own capital. Although we had no significant savings, we were fortunate in that the value of our house in Abingdon had gone up and was well above our current mortgage, so we could probably raise some capital by re-mortgaging the house. Jacquie was hugely supportive and urged me to go for it.

First thing the following Monday, two days after reading the RSC accounts, I telephoned Dr Tom Inch, their General Secretary, who was always in his office by 8am. I explained my idea of forming a company which would include in its remit a new LGC/RSC national centre for analytical science, and asked him whether the Society would be willing to invest. Tom had had an interesting career at the chemical defence establishment at Porton and with BP before he joined the RSC. Direct, and not one for suffering fools gladly, he was a surprising choice to run a professional society, but he was certainly effective at getting things done. Although at that stage we had met on only a few occasions, we had had friendly exchanges. I certainly admired his determination to sweep away some of the cobwebs of the Society.

Tom was immediately enthusiastic about the proposal I put to him and agreed to discuss it with the Society's President, Professor Howard Purnell. I did not know Howard well; my wife and I had met him and his wife at a dinner of the RSC's Analytical Division where he and I (together with Mary Archer, wife of the then London Mayoral candidate, Jeffrey Archer) gave after-dinner speeches. His speech was informative and hugely entertaining and when I subsequently invited him to LGC I was struck by his engaging personality, enthusiasm and humour as well as his intellect and shrewd awareness of business. I couldn't have been more fortunate; the RSC's leadership at the time I approached them was receptive and enthusiastic. Within 24 hours I had received a positive response and took Patrick Cook and Matthew Young from 3i to meet Tom Inch at the RSC's headquarters in Burlington House. I then immediately sent a rather formal letter to the DTI permanent secretary, Sir Peter Gregson, informing him of my intention to form a consortium, to include its management and staff, to bid for the purchase of the Laboratory.

The possibility of a new bid to consider alongside the indicative offers which had already been received and the Company Limited by Guarantee option was welcomed by DTI. Their main concern was my involvement and whether I was compromised, but after I had been questioned closely by DTI officials, I received a letter allowing me six weeks to prepare a full bid. I asked whether I might have some support from DTI for professional advice, but officials there said I would have to make a submission to the Treasury for this. Given that this was the first time a civil servant (albeit one on a fixed term contract) had launched a management buy-out bid for a government agency, I knew that this would take ages for them to consider further, so I decided to go it alone and try to do as much as possible myself with no financial support from DTI.

In preparing my bid, a priority was to get some legal advice, and Paul Winson, one of the external members of our steering board, suggested that I should contact David Haggett, the managing partner of Eversheds, based in Birmingham. I telephoned David who, it transpired, did much of his work from his chauffeur-driven Jaguar. He was in his car in central London when we spoke and he agreed to interrupt his work (negotiating terms for rugby players, I seem to recall) and meet me within a couple of hours in Teddington for a sandwich lunch.

The moment David walked into my office I knew that we would get on well. As I was to discover, David was a great raconteur and during my explanation of the position of the Agency and my proposal for a management buy-out he would periodically butt in with some anecdote of a previous transaction he'd been involved in. He seemed to share my left-of-centre political leanings and to understand my wish to enable staff to have a substantial stake in the company. He had pioneered the concept of management buy-outs as a consequence of some appalling examples of ownership and management he had seen in engineering companies in the West Midlands. During our discussion he likened the management challenges of running a scientific laboratory to those of his law firm and he gave me a lecture on taxation and the importance of getting the structure of any transaction right to minimise any future tax liabilities. By the end of our meeting he had agreed to help me and said that his assistant, Sue Lewis, would work for me. David didn't like to discuss money – that, apparently, was a matter for Sue – but he indicated that he wouldn't charge for his initial support in the preparation of the bid.

Meanwhile, although I had received enthusiastic backing from the leadership of the Royal Society of Chemistry, Tom Inch and Howard Purnell, it became clear that getting the approval of the Society as a whole would not be straightforward. Tom decided to ask the Council of the Society to set up a working party to examine my proposal, including the Laboratory's viability, the legal implications and the effect on RSC members who worked for competing laboratories. Shrewdly, he appointed Dr Roy Jeffries OBE, a retired director of Kodak and the RSC's Honorary Treasurer as chairman. Roy's good-humoured and enthusiastic approach was counterbalanced by the inclusion on the working party of one or two of those most doubtful of the proposal. However, the secretary of the working party, Martin Hunt, who was Tom Inch's right-hand man, proved an invaluable channel of communication and I was kept fully informed of the group's progress over the coming months.

Work on a full offer document and business plan began immediately. I had privately discussed my proposal with the Laboratory's senior staff. Although his secondment was coming to an end, John Reynolds was very supportive and it was agreed he would stay as DTI's representative until the Laboratory of the Government Chemist was sold, either to a trade bidder or to my 'consortium'. The finance manager, Adrian Wilson, later to become LGC's first finance director, backed the bid, as did Roy Dietz, although he was on the brink of retirement. Other senior managers were less certain, but I gathered together a group of middle managers whom I thought most likely to be supportive. While not fully understanding what was involved, they reacted enthusiastically.

Chapter 2 My management buy-out

Suddenly there was a vast amount of work to do and DTI made it clear that the preparation of my bid had to be done in my 'free' time. I obviously had to continue the day-to-day management of the Agency but the whole of July was also taken up with laying the groundwork for my bid. Adrian Wilson, who was enthusiastic about my plans from the outset, helped with approaches for debt finance from banks, and we approached two pension providers – Equitable Life and Scottish Widows – to prepare proposals for a pension scheme to replace the civil service scheme to which almost all members of staff belonged. We asked Coopers and Lybrand to examine the financial forecasts that we produced.

From a personal point of view, having to prepare an offer document over July and August was not ideal. Jacquie and I had booked a holiday in France in August and we had made arrangements with our supportive doctor and his wife and Helen House, the children's hospice we had helped to found, for our daughter Helen to be cared for during this period so that we could have a relaxing time with our other young daughters, Catherine and Isobel. It would have been deeply unfair on my family to cancel the holiday which was a chance, particularly for Jacquie, to have a break from the relentlessly demanding care of Helen. However, I knew that the eyes of 3i would be on me and that I had to prove to them that I was fully committed to the management buy-out bid.

It is hard to recall the age before mobile phones and laptops, but in 1995 I didn't have a 'carphone', and faxes, usually on long rolls of photosensitive paper, were the fastest way of transmitting written material. I hired a phone for the period of my holiday so that I could keep in touch with my office, and arranged for documents to be faxed to the post office in the French village nearest the rural gîte we had rented. I was able to spend time writing the business plan and communicating with 3i without them being too aware of my absence from my desk. Given that I was writing most of the text myself, being away from my office gave me the chance to plan the shape of the new company I proposed to form.

The letter I delivered to DTI on 6 September 1995 headed 'Proposal for the purchase of the Laboratory of the Government Chemist by a company to be formed by the Royal Society of Chemistry, 3i Group plc and the management and staff of the Laboratory' was accompanied by a business plan. This plan set out my vision for the business and how the DTI's objectives for the sale, including the need to maintain the statutory role of the Government Chemist and to safeguard the Laboratory's reputation for independence and impartiality, would be met. It provided detailed sales forecasts and discussed the Laboratory's competitive position. The financial forecasts included capital requirements and there was detailed consideration of property issues surrounding the Teddington site of the Laboratory. Appendices included letters of support I had elicited from 3i, The Royal Society of Chemistry, NatWest Markets, The Association of Public Analysts and the British Measurement and Testing Association.

The consideration of human resource issues in the bid was quite detailed. I had always been interested in staff engagement, motivation and productivity, and over the years had read widely and been to occasional seminars on the subject, including with the chairman of the retailer John Lewis Partnership, with organisations promoting staff share ownership, with the Work Foundation (then the Industrial Society) and with trade union representatives. The business plan for the new company was my chance to set out clearly my beliefs about management and staff engagement.

Although I recognised that senior managers would be expected to buy shares and put their personal money at risk (details were given of nine managers who were willing to do this), I wanted to encourage the ongoing financial participation of all staff. I had always respected the tenets of the co-operative movement, but it was disappointing that the management of co-operatives was often rather feeble. The John Lewis model had been more successful and there were several entrepreneurial companies where staff share ownership was a key ingredient of their achievement. In the field of professional services there are many highly successful partnerships. My initial plan proposed a share option scheme and a Save as You Earn (SAYE) share purchase scheme, although this was later adapted to include an Employee Benefit Trust. The bid indicated that, although the transfer of staff to the new company would be covered by Transfer of Undertaking and Protection of Employment (TUPE) legislation, new employment terms and conditions would have to be introduced, but that this would not be done until there had been full consultation. I also made clear that the smaller public sector trades unions representing very small numbers of staff would be de-recognised and that just one union, the

Institution of Professional Managers and Specialists (IPMS) (now called Prospect), would be recognised to represent staff interests. I also made clear that I would want to consider the possible introduction of a 'works council' at which issues affecting all staff (not just union members) could be discussed.

The share structure of the offer aimed to support the independence and impartiality of the company by ensuring that none of the three participants in the 'consortium' would have a majority. I also proposed that the board should include a non-executive chairman and two other non-executive directors with me as chief executive and probably just one other executive director.

The actual offer for the business and assets of the Laboratory of the Government Chemist was £5 million. (David insisted that this should be written in full and in bold!) The plan indicated that this would be funded from £600,000 of shares divided equally between the three groups, £1.4 million of preference shares to be owned by 3i and RSC and £3 million loan finance. However, the offer was subject to several conditions, including the offer of a clawback provision in the sale of the freehold of the Teddington building so that, in the unlikely event of the building being sold within an agreed period, the government would receive a proportion of the sale price over the purchase price. Other conditions related to some site works and the cost of the possible further reduction in staffing levels; these were set out in the plan.

Although my letter was formally acknowledged, it seemed an age (though it was probably only a couple of weeks) before I got any real feedback, which came in the form of supplementary questions. The fact that I was being asked further questions gave me hope that the offer was being seriously considered. In the meantime, the RSC working party was beavering away and asking lots of questions and Adrian Wilson and I were receiving presentations from potential pension providers and banks.

At the same time, there were important developments in our business. With the impending privatisation, HM Customs & Excise had decided to put out to tender, and market test, the work that we had carried out for them for years on tariff classification and forensic analysis of illicit drugs. Up to then, the Laboratory had undertaken this work on a cost plus basis; now we were being asked to prepare a proposal against a very detailed tender specification which required price lists for all services. Our accounting systems did not provide the information that we needed to price our bid and those involved had little experience of pricing decisions. The tender document we submitted in November was impressive, but I was unsure as to whether we had got the pricing right. Another more minor management issue was around the future of our outstation at Botley, Hampshire which had remained following the closure of our Gosport Laboratory. The Botley unit was no longer viable and we decided to close it and move the residual work to Teddington.

After frequent telephone discussions with DTI officials and their consultants from PA, I received a message that, while not making any firm commitment, DTI would like to draft a 'heads of terms' agreement. Tom Inch from RSC, Patrick Cook from 3i and I were invited to a meeting at which we were asked about board representation and the proposed structure of the company and Tom and Patrick were questioned on what due diligence their respective organisations would require.

Things began to move swiftly. 3i suggested that it would be sensible to appoint a shadow non-executive director to help in the formation of the company, and they put forward three names for me to consider. Having studied their cvs, I interviewed two of them. My first meeting with Dennis Stocks, was slightly strange. A blunt Lancastrian, he began by emphasising that, while he had been the '3i director' on several boards he refused to be labelled as such since he was independent and acted in the company's, and not solely in the shareholders', interests. Dennis's cv recorded that following his graduation, two years working for ICI had taught him everything he knew about management and how not to do it!

I liked Dennis's directness and, while I suspected he thought I was a soft southerner, I instinctively knew that we would work well together and that he would be in tune with the company I wanted to create. His experience of management buy-outs, including his own of a chemical company, and of corporate transactions, would be invaluable. It was agreed that Dennis would provide advice when necessary during the negotiation process and he accompanied me to some key meetings with DTI. 3i agreed to underwrite a fee of £12,000, which the company would pay if it was successful, and to pay Dennis's expenses. I learned that Dennis was extremely economical, taking buses rather than taxis except when accompanied by his wife, Wendy, when he would then claim just half of the taxi fare!

A particular hurdle that had to be cleared was the approval of the structure for the transaction which David Haggett had proposed, in which DTI would form a company with a single share to which the assets and liabilities of the Laboratory of the Government Chemist would be transferred; my company, funded by the 'consortium' would then purchase the share. This would enable the new company to have the independently assessed value of the Teddington building on its balance sheet without an immediate capital gains tax liability. I was not party to the discussion which took place between DTI and the Treasury, but the consortium's offer was approved early in November. This paved the way for an announcement by Ian Taylor MP, DTI's Minister of State responsible for Science and Technology, that my 'consortium' had been selected as the 'preferred bidder' and that it was planned that the sale would be completed by the end of January.

Negotiations rapidly intensified. The main Agreements covering the privatisation were to be: the central sale and purchase agreement; a 'framework agreement' under which DTI would place contracts for an initial five years covering the Government Chemist function, work in support of consumer safety and the Laboratory's contribution to the National Measurement System; and an agreement between DTI, the company and the Royal Society of Chemistry covering the continued expertise and independence of the Government Chemist. However, there were numerous other agreements to cover – among other matters, the land, buildings and rights of way, the supply of heating from the Teddington site district heating scheme, the transfer of staff under TUPE and the re-appointment of myself as Government Chemist.

Although I led all the negotiations myself, I asked Dr John Mason, who had worked for me during my time at Harwell and whom I had recruited to LGC a couple of years before, to help with the 'Framework Agreement' covering the commercial terms of the Laboratory's work for DTI. Ian Van Nierop, who was the site manager and who had previously been involved in the construction of the Teddington building, provided dogged support with site and building matters. Adrian Wilson helped with the financial terms and in setting up the new pension scheme, while our head of human resources worked on staffing matters. John Reynolds, although he would return to DTI once privatisation had been achieved, provided invaluable help with these and many other issues and in smoothing the way with DTI. Sue Lewis, with whom I was in daily contact, led a team from Eversheds covering the commercial agreements, the building agreements, and staffing matters, including management contracts.

Dennis Stocks and David Haggett accompanied me to some of the key negotiations, where they were often able to unblock things by adopting a more detached position, and they were always available for advice and sometimes much-needed moral support. David recommended some changes to the employee share scheme and suggested that my vision of staff share ownership could better be accomplished if I established an 'employee benefit trust' which would also enable limited sales and purchases of staff shares, for example when staff left the company.

Although the negotiations were conducted in a totally commercial manner, one aspect was fundamentally different. Normally in a negotiation there are trade-offs where one side gives ground on one point in exchange for gaining something on another point. In these negotiations, mindful of criticisms which had been levelled after previous privatisations, and knowing that the National Audit Office would ultimately review the whole process, the DTI had to be able to justify each and every part of the Agreements. This led to interminably long meetings where Sue Lewis and I would face DTI officials and their lawyer, Martin Mendlessohn, a partner in McKenna (now Cameron McKenna), going though Agreements clause by clause and arguing every point.

The issue of pensions was critical. For civil servants, their final salary pension was an essential part of their contract with their employer. Even if pay was not great, at that time if you stuck the course you could retire aged 60 with a lump sum and an index-linked pension for the rest of your life relating to your years of service and your final salary. Adrian Wilson and I approached two pension providers who offered schemes which essentially mirrored the civil service scheme. With agreement from DTI we provided them with anonymised details of staff, their salaries and age. At the end of November we received two proposals, one from Scottish Widows and the other from Equitable Life. Even after taking independent actuarial advice from Coopers & Lybrand, it appeared to us to be a very even contest, but there was something which we preferred about the Scottish Widows proposal, even though Equitable Life played strongly their card as the world's oldest and most respected life assurer. (They had Standard & Poor's AA rating and were quoted as providing excellent financial security.) Frankly, it was more by luck than by skill that we decided to appoint Scottish Widows and thereby avoid the consequences of the near collapse of Equitable Life which was to occur at the end of 1999. With DTI we engaged in discussions with the Government Actuary and arranged extensive presentations to all staff of the new pension scheme. It was many months after the transaction that a value was agreed for accrued pensions and transfers were made to the new scheme.

The question of banking was more straightforward. We approached banks asking them for acquisition loan, overdraft and other banking facilities and provided them with our business plan and other documents. We received very full presentations from NatWest Markets and Midland Bank, soon to be rebranded as HSBC. Their offers were similar, but Adrian and I agreed just before Christmas that we would prefer to work with HSBC. It was the beginning of a long and very fruitful relationship. I was now confident that we would have access to sufficient financial resources to launch the new company and work began on drafting the memorandum and articles of association for the company which was to become LGC (Holdings) Ltd. Adrian Wilson and I were the initial shareholders.

In the meantime, the position of the RSC was becoming difficult. They had to make a submission to the Privy Council to establish that a shareholding in LGC, a private company, was permitted under their Royal Charter. This required advice from their lawyers and took time. However, a more fundamental difficulty was gaining agreement from within the Society itself and, in particular, addressing the concerns of a small but vocal group within the membership of 40,000 or so. After considering a detailed interim report from the working party and examining a wide range of issues, including financial risk and conflict of interest, the RSC Council agreed at a meeting on 7 December 1995, which I attended, to go ahead with its investment, subject to the completion of the lengthy due diligence process. However, opposition within RSC's membership intensified, with letters and petitions being submitted. In response, the RSC decided to call an open consultation meeting scheduled for 23 January 1996 to which 1140 members considered to have a special interest were invited. In normal circumstances the meeting would have been chaired by the President, Professor Howard Purnell. However, sadly he was critically ill (he died the following month) and it was chaired by the previous President, Professor Charles Rees, who had been less involved with the proposed transaction. The 80 members who attended argued vociferously that the RSC should never have become involved with LGC and should not risk their money by investing in my company. Tom Inch, members of the RSC working party, and I, who were on the platform with Professor Rees, attempted to explain the nature of the agreement between my putative company and the RSC and to address the concerns which were raised. However, the meeting became increasingly hostile, with members accusing the RSC of failing to consult more widely. I listened with disbelief as Professor Rees finally agreed to a demand that the RSC should ballot its entire membership.

I left the meeting feeling shattered that my concept of a company in which the RSC would have a role protecting the impartiality of the Government Chemist and promoting analytical science appeared to have been destroyed. The sale process had already been delayed, but a poll of the RSC membership would take months. That evening I had a long discussion with Jacquie. She was as frustrated as I was about the RSC but urged me not to give up but to go ahead without them if necessary. Plan B would be to set up an independent advisory group to take RSC's 'custodian' role; with a gradual erosion of the offer price which I had achieved during negotiation, the RSC's role as an investor was no longer essential.

The following morning I went straight to Tom Inch's office in Burlington House and told him that, unless the RSC abandoned the idea of a ballot of its members within 24 hours, I would go ahead without them being part of the consortium. Tom fully understood why a ballot at this stage was out of the question and promised to get the project back on track. The RSC agreed to invite seven of those most opposed to the RSC's involvement with LGC to attend a full Council meeting on 15 February where they would be allowed to put forward their objections. The bulky report of the due-diligence audit conducted by the RSC Working Party entitled '*Guarding the Integrity of the Government Chemist & the LGC*', was presented at the meeting. The Council then met in closed session where they concluded that no issues not previously considered had been raised and voted by 28 to 1 to uphold the original decision to participate in the purchase of LGC. All this was duly recorded in reports, correspondence and statements in the Society's monthly magazine, *Chemistry in Britain*. So, after several weeks of chaos, during which I had tried at all times to appear confident to DTI officials, things appeared to be back on track.

The RSC's position was not the only threat to my company before it had finally been formed. Another cause for delay was the uncertain outcome of the HMCE tender. My bid had said that, if LGC failed to retain this work, we would reduce the offer by the cost of the consequent redundancies. It became clear that the outcome was in the balance. Despite pressure from DTI, HMCE stuck to their guns; the successful privatisation of LGC was not part of their remit. During one of the lengthy negotiating sessions with DTI, we heard 'off the record' the news that HM Customs and Excise were not going to award LGC the contract for drugs analysis work. The Forensic Science Service had submitted a keenly priced bid and HMCE were likely to award at least part of the new contract to them. This represented a substantial loss in business and was a heavy blow at this late stage. Although we were to appeal against this decision, and DTI did their best to change it, I knew that it was unlikely to be reversed. At the eleventh hour, with Sue Lewis from Eversheds, we proposed a clause in our agreements which would require DTI to cover the cost of redundancies in the event of the HMCE contract not being awarded.

There were also issues with other agreements. The title of the land and building we were purchasing was not straightforward. Some of the land was in a part of Bushy Park which had been 'clapperstile allotments', leased to the Park in periods of 33 years. (Apparently this was an ancient device to prevent the King selling off the family silver.) There were disputes over rights of access and a requirement on LGC to move a building. In hindsight, leaving aside the delays caused by the RSC, it is not surprising that it took until the end of March before all the agreements were ready to be signed.

A more amusing issue was the question of the use of the Laboratory of the Government Chemist's name and trade mark. Michael Heseltine had at the outset recognised the importance of our being able to continue to use our name, The Laboratory of the Government Chemist, and the DTI lawyers subsequently confirmed that it was possible for a private sector company to include 'Government' (a so-called 'sensitive word' in company registration) in its name. However, our logo, a crown on top of a schematic representation of a set of scales (representing the position of the Government Chemist as referee analyst in legal cases) was a different matter. The logo was used very widely; it was on just about every bottle in laboratories, it was used on every report or certificate that we produced, and it was even etched on a huge mirror in the lift.

The DTI made an approach to the Lord Chamberlain's office which was, apparently, in charge of authorising the use of the crown, but the response was that the crown could not be used by a company in the private sector. Mindful of the cost of removing the crown immediately from everywhere it was used, I asked DTI if I could make an approach myself. I telephoned Buckingham Palace and was put through to a senior official in the Lord Chamberlain's Department. I explained that the Laboratory of the Government Chemist was to be privatised and that it would be owned partly by the Royal Society of Chemistry. During a long conversation I was regaled with views on how wrong it was that the Post Office might be privatised and that the privatisation of the railways was a mistake. As a long standing republican it felt strange to be listening to the opinions of a royalist who was clearly unhappy with any change. On the other hand, he seemed sympathetic to my request that LGC, with a history stretching back over a century and a half, should continue to be able to use its logo and he agreed to write to DTI to that effect. Though this was perhaps a minor achievement – to have been successful where DTI had failed – I felt rather pleased with myself. In practical terms a trade mark agreement between DTI and LGC would allow us to continue to use our full name and the crown and scales logo, removing the need for an immediate and costly change. However, as it happened, just a year later, our new company decided to change our corporate identity, abandoning the old logo and adopting one more in keeping with modern times.

Negotiations of all the Agreements seemed to be grinding on forever. However, the deadline of the end of March provided the stimulus needed to resolve all the key issues. The signing was to take place on Friday 29th March, and Adrian Wilson and I duly arrived with our pens at the offices of DTI's lawyers, McKennas. Sue Lewis and her assistant from Eversheds were already at work with the lawyers from McKennas, making sure that all the Agreements were arranged in the right order for us to sign. There were just a few final outstanding matters to be resolved, including a clause covering compensation for the potential loss of the HMCE contract. Taking my advice that things would take some time to get ready, Professor Eddie Abel, the newly appointed President of the Royal Society of Chemistry, did not arrive until after lunch but it was early evening before we were able to sign the RSC Agreement and, as token consideration for what was a contract between RSC and DTI, a one pound coin was solemnly handed to Professor Abel. However, there were still many other Agreements to sign, and I sat down with John Hobday and his DTI colleagues to discuss the outstanding points. We struggled to find a way of accommodating potential redundancy costs associated with the probable loss of the HMCE contract and I asked our HR manager to join us. John Hobday, whose hopes of going to Covent Garden that evening were rapidly fading, was then joined by Brian Hilton. The atmosphere was tense when, at 9pm, Patrick Cook from 3i joined our meeting. He provided a fresh voice to reinforce the arguments I was making and we managed to resolve all the remaining differences. We then went on to sign the final Agreements under which the company I had formed, LGC (Holdings) Ltd, would acquire the shares in a company formed by the DTI LGC (Teddington) Ltd (which owned the assets and staff of the Laboratory of the Government Chemist) at one minute to midnight on Sunday 31st March. After a glass of champagne and expressions of thanks all round, I was able to catch the last train back home.

In the early hours of the following morning, exhausted by the events leading up to and during that final day, and too tired to celebrate immediately, I sat down with Jacquie to reflect on all that had happened. The immense effort leading up to this moment had been worth it. My vision of a unique new enterprise, headed by myself and involving all the staff, a private equity company, and a learned society, was now a reality, but where would I take it from here?

Chapter 3: *The new company*

The new company and governance – Staff involvement and share ownership – New business plans – Changing perceptions – First acquisition and expansion of DNA work

At 8am on Monday 1st April 1996 I was at my desk in my office in Teddington in charge of LGC (Holdings) Ltd which had acquired LGC (Teddington) Ltd, with all the assets and liabilities of the Laboratory of the Government Chemist, at midnight the night before. The company I had worked so hard to create was now a reality. The DTI logo, which had been mounted in huge letters on the side of our splendid Teddington laboratory, was removed and an informal celebration of our move from the public to the private sector was hastily arranged. At lunchtime, in the atrium of the building, everyone was offered a glass of champagne and I gave a short speech thanking staff for their support. There were people to phone, letters to write, and a celebratory reception at the Apothecaries' Hall to arrange for our customers and all those involved in our privatisation.

We issued a press release about the formation of the new company, which prompted several articles in the national and trade press. These included a feature by the respected science journalist Tim Radford in The Guardian entitled 'The man with the biggest chemistry set' which was headed by a picture of me holding up a chemical flask. David Fishlock, the former science correspondent of the Financial Times, devoted one of his newsletters to LGC's privatisation. After all the rather negative publicity about the privatisation of the DTI laboratories, it was refreshing to see articles which took a positive stance. But there were more fundamental things to be done and changes to be made.

During the weeks leading up to privatisation, I had taken steps to form a new board. Dennis Stocks had been closely involved in some of the negotiations and was 3i's nominee as a non-executive director, and the Royal Society of Chemistry had put forward Professor Jack Betteridge as their representative and guardian of the Royal Society of Chemistry Agreement. It had taken some time to find a suitable chairman and it was rather late in the day when my colleague Roy Dietz suggested Brian (later Sir Brian) Richards, co-founder of British Biotechnology, then a successful high-profile company. We had been to see him at his house near Oxford. Having obtained the agreement of the other shareholders, I invited Brian to become LGC's first non-executive chairman. The shadow board (which included myself and Adrian Wilson as executive directors) had met during the last week of March, just before the final deal was done.

The first matters to get straight were procedural. The new board agreed that it would generally meet each month when it would consider regular reports from the chief executive, financial statements and, since safety was essential to our operations, a statement on safety. Delegated financial and contractual powers were established and Brian Richards and Dennis Stocks proposed that the new company should adopt the Cadbury Rules for corporate governance. Corporate governance was a very topical issue. I was mindful of the company's responsibility towards government (which was to remain the dominant customer for some time) but, more generally, felt that proper accountability and transparency were essential ingredients in the type of company I wanted to create. So we heartily endorsed a proposal to adopt 'high standards' of corporate governance and agreed that, although we were a private company, we would produce annual reports and accounts in the form adopted by the best public limited companies. Accordingly, the board established committees to cover audit, appointments and remuneration, with proper terms of reference. I sent formal letters of appointment to the three non-executive directors.

Another formal matter to consider was the relationship with the Royal Society of Chemistry, now covered by formal agreements with DTI and the company. An Advisory Committee needed to be established. The membership was drawn largely from the working party which had carried out the due diligence audit, but Tom Inch proposed that Brian Pierce, then President of the RSC Analytical Division should chair it. The Advisory Committee was to meet four times a year and I attended as an observer and to provide a report on LGC's activities.

There were numerous other administrative questions which occupied Adrian Wilson's time, not least the appointment of Trustees for the pension fund, the appointment of auditors, and finalising arrangements for the staff share option scheme and employee benefit trust. However, perhaps top of the list was agreeing with DTI the final closing accounts for the Agency. In several other privatisations, the closing accounts led to bitter arguments (in one case, the accounts took more than two years to settle), but Adrian's diligence and quiet diplomacy ensured that there were no disputes. The accounts, signed by DTI and laid before Parliament in October, were certified by the Comptroller and Auditor General to the House of Commons and included a report by the National Audit Office on the privatisation, which gave all parties a totally clean bill of health. My statement at the front of the report and accounts noted that, although there was a relatively small loss in 1995/6, this followed several years of strong financial performance as an Agency. I expressed confidence that LGC had been transferred to the private sector in such a way that we would be able to build on, and strengthen, our reputation as a national centre for analytical science and that we would continue to flourish. So this rather plain and formal document signed off 154 years in the public sector and six years as an Agency, leaving good will on all sides.

However, important though it was, getting procedures and paper work straight was not the main issue. The crucial tasks were to win new work, to restore profitability and to develop a blueprint for the type of company we wanted to become. I had always been interested in the dynamics of the work place and how successful organisations, especially technical organisations, were managed. Early in my management career I had visited a number of European companies with the European Industrial Research Management Association. I had also been invited by Brunel University to present, at a course they were running, a case study on matrix management of R&D functions based on my experiences at Harwell; Tom McKillop presented another case study based on his experiences at ICI. During my time as part of DTI I had attended seminars given to small groups of senior civil servants by business leaders. Listening to John Birt I could understand why he had lost the respect of BBC employees, but I was inspired by Stuart Hampton, a former civil servant and subsequently Chairman of The John Lewis Partnership, who gave a fascinating account of the involvement of all staff in their highly successful retail business.

Before setting up our staff share ownership scheme, I had looked at a number of models for connecting staff with the objectives of the business. Our Project PRIME (concerned with changing our performance and reward management from the civil service system), which had been initiated in the run-up to privatisation, presented a chance to mould a new culture for the organisation. This new performance management system required all staff, up to and including me, to agree objectives at the start of each year, which related to the overall objectives of the business. Progress against these objectives was reviewed during the year and assessed at the end of the year. In this way, staff had regular reviews with their line manager, and there were various checks to ensure this took place. However, inevitably, some managers were more conscientious than others in looking after their staff, and other means of communication were necessary to ensure that no one was left out in the cold.

I had always supported the team briefing system promoted by the Industrial Society (later to become the Work Foundation) and I introduced team briefing which involved providing a 'core brief' each month which was cascaded down the management chain, with local briefing material being added at each level. The briefing involved face-to-face contact with managers who were trained in how to deliver the brief; some were excellent, others found it a bit of a struggle. Together with our staff newsletter, LGC News, team briefing was one of the many means I adopted for communicating new messages to staff.

Communication is a crucial element in managing change in an organisation. One of the most common barriers to changing an organisation is the 'middle management' who may themselves feel threatened by changes over which they feel they have little real control. Intelligent scientists are often cynical of initiatives which they may feel have little relevance to their 'real' work. My response was to try to meet with small groups of staff, usually eight or ten at a time, whom I invited to sandwich lunches. I would usually ask them to bring topics for discussion, harnessing an idea my wife had used with her students and as Chair of BBC Radio Oxford's Advisory Council, that each 'brickbat' should be matched with a 'bouquet' so that the discussion did not become simply a moan about what was wrong.

Although I also addressed larger groups of staff regularly, these small less formal meetings were a way of explaining directly, to staff at all levels, what was going on, and receiving direct feedback from all parts of the company.

Initially I held these lunchtime meetings with team leaders, usually themselves responsible for up to twenty or so staff within their team. We would sit round the boardroom table and talk about the company. At first, much of the discussion at such meetings was on internal management issues, but gradually the focus changed to broader discussions of the business environment and prospects for development. The opportunity for rather conservative managers to meet others with more imaginative ideas, some of whom had joined the company from other organisations, was itself a catalyst for change. It also helped break down a barrier that existed between scientific staff and those in service departments such as marketing and finance. In time I altered the format of these meetings to include staff at different levels; it was often the more junior staff who put forward ideas and proposals to improve the company. Finding the time to talk directly to staff was not always easy, but I tried to impose a discipline on myself not only to hold regular lunchtime meetings but also to engage in 'management by walking about'. I regularly visited offices and laboratories informally, without prior arrangement, and talked to staff about their work. I found these visits very informative; I was able to get feedback from staff at all levels as well as to explain why various management actions were being taken. I enjoyed the conversations I had and they invariably sparked off ideas for improving the organisation.

Full-time employees spend half their waking hours at work during a typical working day and, although no one can expect all their time at work to be satisfying and enjoyable, I believe strongly that providing worthwhile jobs and making the work environment as congenial as possible is not only fulfilling for the individual but a major contributor to the success of the enterprise. An organisation wants the commitment of its staff but it also has to accommodate work/life balance priorities which will vary between individuals. LGC is fortunate in that its work (such as ensuring food is safe or helping to solve crimes) is demonstrably for the public good, so that staff can be proud of their work and can talk about it freely (subject to any commercial confidentiality) to friends and acquaintance. In motivating staff, reward (possibly including share ownership) and career opportunities are important, but equally important is a culture of mutual respect and feeling part of a team. Creating such a culture in an organisation made up of intelligent, creative and cynical people is a challenge. With all his management consultants, John Birt evidently failed at the BBC whereas, until crisis struck, Greg Dyke seemed to be winning the hearts and minds of staff there. There is obviously no single recipe for success but (perhaps because I am an amateur violinist) I tried to adopt the style of leadership found in a chamber music orchestra where, after much rehearsal, a nod from the leader ensures a perfectly harmonised performance. I had never enjoyed working for dictatorial or remote bosses and tried to be different, feeling that it was more effective in the longer term to spend time on explanation and persuasion, although there were obviously times when decisions had to be made which did not necessarily gain support from everyone.

In this context, I have always been a supporter of 'away days' when the management team meet away from the normal workplace to discuss questions of policy. Such conferences need careful preparation and are not necessarily the occasion for management decision-making but, if handled well, they can be a valuable way of exploring options and engendering a team spirit. So, six weeks after the company had come into being, the management team met for two days in May at the nearby Petersham Hotel in Richmond. I gave a short talk to set the scene and the heads of divisions in the new management structure each gave short presentations on how they intended to develop their business areas.

We discussed our business model – essentially two areas, one focused on our 'national centre' role, providing support for international standards and government programmes, and the other focused on analytical services. Our total turnover of £14.5 million for our final year as an Agency was divided equally between these two areas and we considered how each area might develop. Some of the contracts within the 'national centre' had been underpinned by the DTI for 5 years but we expected these contracts to be reduced thereafter; however, we were optimistic about building up other activities to compensate, and even increasing the size of this activity. We could only guess what might be possible for the three 'commercial' divisions – food, environment and forensic. Instinctively we felt there were good opportunities with the food industry and supermarkets and we noted the opportunity for doing forensic work for the police, which we were beginning to explore. With very little experience of the markets but fired up by Ray Ah-Sun, who was in the lead in developing 'new ventures', we optimistically set ourselves the target of expanding current commercial services by 100%. If we achieved this, our total turnover would increase from £14.5 million to £22 million by 2001 and, since the high fixed costs associated with our operations would not change with a higher volume of work, our profitability should increase substantially.

It was on the basis of these estimates that we formulated our first 'corporate strategy' which I presented to all staff. I also decided to prepare a small booklet explaining the management and ownership structure of the company, our vision, our business strategy and our markets. Our privatisation had been complicated and I felt it was important to try to spell out all aspects of our new status to staff at every level and to explain as far as I could what plans we were formulating for the future. All staff were given a copy of the booklet, *'LGC: Organisation and Strategy'* which I introduced at one of my regular series of talks to staff.

In preparing our first year's budget, rather late in the day and already several weeks into the financial year, we took a cautious view of our ability to generate new business quickly, but we took an even more cautious approach to expenditure. I was determined to be as economical with overheads as possible. Partly as a symbol, senior staff gave up the right to first-class travel which they had had as civil servants and, when the car park was rearranged, we abandoned the reserved spaces which had been associated with civil service grades. All staff were urged to be economical in the use of resources, but I emphasised that we would use the money saved to invest in the future. I was delighted that during our first quarter the board approved expenditure (of over £400,000) on the largest capital purchase of an analytical instrument (an advanced inductively coupled plasma mass spectrometer) that we had ever made.

Purchasing a much-needed new telephone system was less straightforward. Our building manager was used to public procurement processes where suppliers were asked to tender against a specification which he produced. On this occasion, we persuaded him to change the process. The specification was closely examined and simplified and then suppliers were given a certain freedom to make changes and suggest economies.

Tough negotiations ensued with the shortlisted companies and, after a number of iterations, the cost was reduced to a third of the original estimate. The exchange which was finally installed was fully satisfactory. Similarly, we had set money aside from our negotiations with DTI to deal with some essential new building works at our Teddington site, including the demolition of an unoccupied and contaminated building, moving a storage facility for gas cylinders, and constructing an independent boiler house, required to replace the site hot water system which was being closed. We again managed these projects extremely tightly and looked for economies, while not compromising the quality of the work. These were some of many examples where, freed from the requirement to adhere to public sector processes and procedures, LGC was able to adopt new commercial practices more attuned to the size and nature of the organisation.

One area where I was reluctant to make too many economies was on the landscaping of the Teddington site which was necessary after our new building works. I was keen that areas around the main laboratory building should look attractive, for the benefit of staff and visitors and for residents living in houses which came very close to our site. Protecting the budget for garden maintenance, landscaping, and tree and shrub planting, was a constant battle I had with successive finance directors looking for areas where economies could be made, but I was convinced of the importance of an attractive work environment. Nevertheless, in keeping with our spirit of economy, an enterprising member of staff (a shareholder, incidentally) offered to mow the grass on Saturday mornings with a second-hand mower he had acquired, a considerable saving on the rather inefficient firm who had previously been contracted to do lawnmowing.

The entrance to the Teddington laboratory was an attractive atrium, with a modern piece of sculpture, Carbon Black, consisting of 48 identical folded triangular forms, conveying the idea of molecular structures, which had been commissioned from Liliane Lijn for the opening of the building. However, beyond this point visitors were met by a security barrier operated by a guard who sat within a cubicle behind a bullet-proof glass screen. While security was an important issue (which we finally managed to address in other ways), it was also important that an increasing number of visitors should be welcomed by a professional receptionist and have somewhere to wait until their host collected them to take them inside the building. We set aside what seemed at the time to be a large sum to re-design our entrance and create a small but attractive open area for guests. This symbolised the change we were making from being an inward-looking civil service establishment into an outward-facing, customer-focused business.

A particular feature of our entrance hall was a notice board which welcomed the guests who would be visiting that day. The purpose of this board was partly to make guests feel welcome as they entered the building, but also to inform staff when they arrived at work who would be visiting that day, so that they would be aware of the organisations we were now interacting with. It was the job of the security guard the evening before to mount visitors' names on the special notice board. On one occasion an unexpected problem arose when the visitor the following day was from the Child Support Agency (to discuss our work on paternity testing). The security guard was deeply worried that LGC was working with the CSA, since it transpired that he was a target of their enquiries!

Developing new business took time, but Ray Ah-Sun had made some contacts with BP, whose central laboratory quite close by at Sunbury was under review. He had suggested that the small geochemistry department, which analysed core samples from BP's exploration wells from all over the world, might transfer to LGC under an 'outsourcing contract'. There were numerous discussions and visits from BP's management, and, inevitably, questions of employment terms and pensions seemed more difficult than the logistics of managing an outsourced operation, but finally the transfer was agreed. Four key staff left BP and joined LGC and their equipment was moved the few miles down the road to Teddington. Under the agreement, the team would continue to serve BP but would be free to tender for work from other oil exploration companies. In parallel, we were able to recruit a senior BP scientist, Dr Peter Lyne, who had been a team leader in charge of analytical services. This first move into winning private sector work, though not itself that large, was hugely significant. It went extremely well and gave LGC credibility outside government.

Another important early business move was also initiated by Ray. Ray had met Professor Tony Segal, an eminent physician and immunologist at University College London (UCL). With his friend, a lawyer, John Rochman, Tony had founded a spin-off company (the first of several that he initiated) called University Diagnosics Limited (UDL). After a few rather difficult years, UDL had appointed Dr Paul Debenham as its chief executive and had moved from UCL to a science park building attached to the University of the South Bank at Elephant and Castle. Paul had focused the company, then about 20 people, on DNA measurements for paternity testing, cystic fibrosis testing, pig stress genetics, avian sexing, and some defence forensic work but, with a turnover of about £1 million pa, UDL needed an injection of further capital in order to develop further.

LGC had a small team investigating ways of using DNA as an analytical tool. We had provided some services, such as some work for Marks & Spencer establishing that supposedly pure cashmere sweaters in fact contained a large amount of Chinese rabbit fur. We were trying to expand the services we offered, but were finding it difficult; setting up routine services was not something that came easily to our R&D staff. If we acquired a small company such as UDL, we would immediately have a service operation to which to transfer some of our interesting R&D developments.

Ray seemed to have built up a good relationship with Tony Segal and we opened discussions with Tony and John Rochman and, with their agreement, with Paul Debenham. The timing seemed to be right. Tony and John were keen to cash in on their successful investment and Paul could immediately see the attraction of joining forces with LGC. Ray and I handled the negotiations, which were kept very secret within LGC and given the code name of 'Springbok', a reference to Tony Segal's South African background. The negotiations were completely different from those I had had with DTI which had seemed to go on for ever. The vendors were looking to be paid £1M, but we were mindful of the risks inherent in UDL's business, and we wanted to conserve as much cash as possible, as we felt this would be needed for future investment in the business. Quite speedily we agreed on a figure of £630K. The due diligence took rather longer, and several tense weeks were spent with our lawyers, Eversheds, led, as in our transaction with DTI, by Sue Lewis. Having dealt with a few skeletons in the cupboard, we had to put our offer to, it transpired, 30 or so private shareholders who had also invested in UCL. The offer document was probably as long and complicated as if we had been taking over a major plc; we were pleased when it was finally accepted and the Daily Telegraph published a news report on the front of their business pages with a picture of Paul Debenham and me with parrots sitting on our shoulders. The use of DNA to determine the sex of parrots was a gift of a story for publicity purposes, even though it was not a particularly profitable part of the business!

Although LGC's purchase of UDL was not formally completed until February 1997, Paul Debenham had effectively been working with us for several months. Aware of the huge interest in DNA as a forensic tool, and the enormous backlog in samples awaiting analysis at the Home Office Forensic Science Service (FSS), we identified forensic applications of DNA as a potential major opportunity for LGC. The previous summer, a few months after the launch of the new company, I had been to see the Home Office and, subsequently, had visited Ben Gunn, the Chief Constable of Cambridgeshire, and Don Dovaston, Deputy Chief Constable of Derbyshire, who both had particular responsibility within the Association of Chief Police Officers (ACPO) for forensic science. I had never met senior police officers before and was certainly surprised by the experience. Ben Gunn was incredibly easy to get on with and seemed very supportive of the idea of LGC offering DNA services in competition to the FSS which, he admitted, had a mixed reputation within police forces. Over lunch at a subsequent meeting with Paul, Ray and me, he regaled us with the story of his arrest for speeding by officers from his own force! Don Dovaston was a complete contrast. After he had given us an hour-long grilling, a junior colleague and I felt we understood what it was to be interviewed in a police station on suspicion of a serious crime. However, Don then changed tack completely and invited us both for lunch in a local Derbyshire pub. Over the meal he encouraged LGC to set up DNA testing facilities as soon as we could. We left feeling wrung out after our interrogation, but optimistic after our lunchtime conversation.

We had received no undertakings that the police would place DNA profiling business with LGC, but it was apparent that, with our close connections with government, we were seen as a credible organisation. On this basis LGC's board approved my proposal that some initial expenditure should be assigned to setting up a DNA profiling laboratory in one of the laboratory wings we had vacated as a consequence of the 'operational review' in the run-up to privatisation. Paul Debenham gave invaluable advice on the layout of this laboratory and Dr Surrinder Johal, a young and enthusiastic microbiologist who had successfully set up and managed our drugs screening laboratory, began to implement the plans. She adapted our Laboratory Information Management System (LIMS) to enable each criminal justice sample to be tracked at every stage of the process with unique bar codes. We subsequently appointed Dr Rita Barallon of our analytical molecular biology research team to manage the laboratory and gain the required accreditation; unbelievably, we were required by the Home Office also to get approval from FSS, the organisation with which we would be competing.

Just a year after my initial meetings with them, but now after the acquisition of UDL and substantial capital investment in the new DNA laboratory, Ben Gunn and Don Dovaston came to Teddington to inspect progress. Our new laboratory facilities were impressive. DNA profiling depends on a process which involves 'amplifying' a very small amount of genetic material before it is analysed in a sequencer. The worry is that a tiny amount of contamination of genetic material from another source (from hair from a laboratory technician, for example) can lead to a false result. Although LGC's laboratories had been designed for work with chemicals – with air extraction systems to remove solvents and other hazards – it was relatively easy to adapt the ventilation systems to minimise the possibility of cross-contamination in genetic measurements. Keeping positive air pressure in the corridor which separated laboratories ensured that the risk of genetic material passing from one part of the process to another was very small. Moreover, Paul Debenham introduced a system of differently coloured laboratory coats to help prevent staff inadvertently moving into the wrong area. So, although we had kept costs to a minimum (our initial costs amounted to around £1 million), our facilities were incredibly well designed and were at that time probably as good as, or better than, any other forensic facilities available in Europe.

Shortly after the inspection visits from police forces, we received our first order from Nottinghamshire Police to profile 186 samples. Our reputation for rapid turnaround times and excellent customer service spread quickly and other orders followed. It was a huge relief that our major speculative investment in forensic DNA was paying off and that our new business was developing rapidly. A few months later Sir Paul Condon, Commissioner of the Metropolitan Police accepted my invitation to open the DNA laboratory formally on 28 May 1998, when he gave a very positive speech and our chairman, Sir Brian Richards, reflected thoughtfully on the development of DNA as a diagnostic tool. It was a happy day of celebration for our new company.

The new DNA laboratory took up only some of the space in the Teddington building we had cleared in the run-up to privatisation. We made use of some further laboratory space in an imaginative arrangement with Hewlett Packard (HP) under which LGC provided facilities for training in the use of HP (later to become Agilent) laboratory equipment. Two training laboratories were equipped with HP's latest analytical instruments, and a constant stream of analytical scientists and technicians from across Europe attended training courses there. Although the financial return from rent and provision of services was modest, the training courses provided an important opportunity to promote LGC to a much wider audience. The arrangement continued for several years until our own requirements for space, and changes within Agilent, brought a natural end to an excellent relationship.

Of course, not everything across the business went smoothly and we suffered some setbacks. The Pesticides Safety Directorate (PSD), for whom we had provided analytical services for several years, had suffered a reduction in their budget. It transpired that they were unable to reduce spending at MAFF's Central Science Laboratory, the other main contractor, so our work was reduced disproportionately. (Fortunately, the situation was reversed after a couple of years when our technical investment and excellent customer service persuaded PSD actually to increase their programme at LGC.) Another setback was the loss of a contract with HM Prison Service on drugs screening of prisoners (looking for traces of cannabis, heroin, cocaine, LSD, and other drugs). We had initially set up a highly automated laboratory for testing urine samples as part of the armed services' campaign to reduce the use of drugs by soldiers in active service. This work continued for many years and we had an excellent relationship with the Army who regularly renewed our contract. We had expanded this drugs screening work when we won a contract from the Prison Service, but in this case the relationship with the customer was not always easy and I had expressed concern at being asked to take short cuts in the confirmation of positive samples. I therefore wasn't unduly disappointed when we lost the contract with the Prison Service, even though we were at a stage

The new building for the Laboratory of the Government Chemist at Teddington was opened in 1989.

The 150th anniversary of the Laboratory of the Government Chemist in 1992 was marked by a formal dinner at the Apothecaries' Hall. Sitting at the high table are (from left) Paul Winson (steering board member), Peter Bunyan (Chief Scientist at MAFF), the Rt Hon Edward Leigh MP (Undersecretary of State for Industry), Richard Worswick, Sir Brian Unwin (Chairman of HM Customs & Excise), Tony Lane (Chairman of steering board) and Ron Coleman (Chief Engineer and Scientist at DTI).

The opening of the nursery, Bushy Tails, in 1992 by Sir Peter Gregson (DTI permanent secretary) was an important milestone in providing better facilities for staff.

A visit by the Rt Hon Michael Heseltine MP, President of the Board of Trade, in April 1993 was followed by a series of reviews which led to LGC's privatisation. Helen Parkes explains how DNA can be used in analysis.

When the new company was launched, an article in the Guardian painted a positive picture of the future for LGC. This contrasted with the downbeat press coverage which accompanied the privatisation of the DTI laboratories in general.

The old Laboratory of the Government Chemist logo included the crown and scales motif. With its strapline, the new logo aimed to convey the essence of the company which, at that stage, was almost unknown outside government.

Winning a major contract for the Veterinary Medicines Agency involved fitting out a completely new laboratory in space which we had earlier vacated as part of a cost-cutting operational review.

LGC acquired ICI's analytical services at Runcorn in 1998. After the laboratories were refurbished, I invited Jim Ratcliffe, chief executive of INEOS, to perform a formal opening ceremony in 2001. (From left: John Mason, who directed our North West operations, Jim Ratcliffe, and Richard Worswick.)

Among many industrialists and politicians I invited to LGC were members of the House of Commons Select Committee on Science & Technology. (From left: John Marriott (Government Chemist), Brian Iddon MP, Ian Gibson MP, Tim Catterick and Gavin O'Connor.)

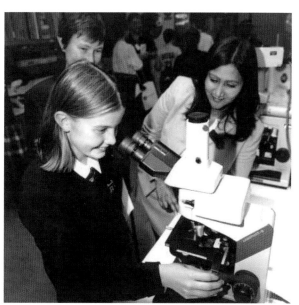

Open days and schools visits were important in promoting chemistry. Selvarani Elahi, a senior food chemist at LGC (right) explains to a visitor how microscopes play an important part in food analysis.

The Annual General Meeting of shareholders was an opportunity for staff shareholders to question the board. (From left: John Beacham (non-executive director), Clive Hall (finance director), Dennis Stocks (non-executive director) Ian Kent (non-executive chairman), Richard Worswick, Marion Sears (non-executive director), John Mason (director, corporate development), and Suzanne Smith (company secretary.)

The opening of a new laboratory at Teddington for the Medicines & Healthcare products Regulatory Agency (MHRA) was the beginning of an important long-term relationship. Lord (Philip) Hunt (2nd from right) formally opened the laboratory in September 2002 .In this photograph he is accompanied by (from left) Paul Debenham, Michael Boardman, Ged Lee (Head of laboratories and licensing at MHRA) and Richard Worswick.

when we really needed to retain everything we could. Finally, although we had developed good relations with food companies and supermarkets such as Tesco, we had not yet managed to land a substantial contract. It was becoming clear that making money by providing quality services to supermarkets was a difficult challenge. Despite these setbacks, we were rapidly learning about new markets. Even though we were not always successful, we probably discovered more about new markets by attempting to make sales than we would have learnt from any amount of market research. Analysing situations is important (and I strongly believe in taking time to consider strategy), but it is actions that move things forward.

During our early days as a company, we had done much to change the culture of our organisation, to make it more customer-focused, and to develop new business. However, we also wanted to change how we were perceived by our customers and suppliers and others with whom we interacted. Although we had a small marketing department, Brian Richards was keen that we should seek help from a PR agency. We approached three firms and asked them to present proposals to the board about how LGC could best present itself. We were particularly impressed by David Lloyd and Mark Thompson from Financial Dynamics (then a relatively small, but now a major, public relations company) and placed a contract with them to work with us on our 'image'. They immediately embarked on a modest but excellent piece of market research. Although we were well respected within government and had a long tradition, it was obvious that there were issues around the name 'Laboratory of the Government Chemist'. The words 'laboratory' and 'chemist' were limiting in terms of our future business and the word 'Government' provoked two opposite reactions. For some, it conveyed the impression of respect and impartiality, for others it represented inefficiency, bureaucracy, a bias in favour of regulation, and conservatism.

We considered a radical change to a completely new name, but we decided there was too much to lose in totally abandoning our past and that we should stick to the abbreviated name 'LGC' rather than use our full trading name, 'The Laboratory of the Government Chemist'. Financial Dynamics also recommended that we should change our logo and harmonise the appearance of our publicity material.

Having previously worked for an organisation that was constantly changing its logo, and knowing how much rebranding exercises could cost, I was anxious not to waste money and go overboard. The design company we chose came up with some simple designs and the management team selected a simple roundel with 'LGC' in the middle. Financial Dynamics felt that we needed a 'strapline' to summarise what 'LGC' represented and they came up with a list of suggestions. Not particularly liking any of them, I turned to my wife, a linguist by background and someone with a creative feel for words, for advice. Sitting in bed one Sunday morning she started making up straplines, selecting key words that conveyed what LGC did. The one she felt fitted best was 'Setting standards in analytical science'. 'Science' rather than 'chemistry' embraced a wider range of activities (including molecular biology) and 'setting standards' not only embraced our national centre role but also positioned us as the leader in the market and suggested quality. The following day I phoned Mark Thompson at Financial Dynamics and asked him to include this in the list of options. Neither of us mentioned that it was Jacquie's suggestion, and it was put to the management team along with a shortlist of suggestions produced by the professionals. It was selected unanimously as the strapline which best put across the message we wanted to convey.

Aware that our staff were finding all the changes at LGC difficult to cope with, I was fearful that the change of logo would be resisted by some of the 'old guard'. Yet it was important that everyone signed up to the new identity. Financial Dynamics helped prepare an explanatory booklet with guidelines on the use of our new corporate identity and, with Mark, I addressed all staff at a single meeting. I need not have worried. The reaction was almost universally positive.

A huge amount had already been achieved in the early days of our company, and even those who had been in the civil service for a long time were starting to feel positive about working in the private sector. At our first Annual General Meeting, which was attended by many of our staff shareholders and all our board, as well as representatives of our institutional shareholders 3i and the RSC, I was able to report that, although our financial performance was not yet stunning, our sales were growing and we were making a small but respectable profit. There was increasing confidence that the new company would be a success.

Chapter 4: *Increasing the pace of change*

Building new business – Establishing LGC in the Northwest – Promoting analytical science – Developing a new business selling chemical standards – Expansion in Europe and acquisition of Promochem – Analysing chemical residues in veterinary products – Opportunities for genetic testing

The steady improvement in the financial results during LGC's early days did not reflect the fundamental and far-reaching changes which were taking place within the company. An organisation previously cushioned within the public sector was now having to seek new opportunities, pre-pare proposals, and relentlessly examine ways of improving efficiency. Freed from the constraints of the civil service and now in charge of my own company, I was convinced that LGC had enormous potential; the challenge for me was to change attitudes and the culture within the organisation. I certainly wanted my company to adhere to some of the core values of the civil service – integrity, accountability and trustworthi-ness – but I aimed to combine these with a more dynamic approach to management, quality, and customer service which emulated the best in the private sector. Developing a focused business strategy for an organi-sation which had traditionally delivered rather a ragbag of services pre-sented a challenge, and to some extent we were opportunistic in our approach to new business, chasing every sales lead. I felt that, through encouraging an entrepreneurial approach and not being over-analytical, we would gain the knowledge and experience of markets which we cur-rently lacked.

However, I was constantly on the lookout for the big idea or major transaction which had the potential to lift the company rapidly from our barely viable position at the point of privatisation. Acquisitions carried risk – probably more than most other business decisions – but they would accelerate the development of our new company and give us an immediate presence in key markets. The acquisition of University Diagnostics and the investment in a new DNA laboratory had transformed our life science and forensic businesses; but there were other business areas I wanted to explore, including environmental science and outsourcing.

LGC's environmental activities were relatively modest. For many years we had had a group undertaking water analysis – swimming pools as well as potable and waste waters – and another small group undertook asbestos analysis. We provided advice on the transport of dangerous goods and on contaminated land. With the public's increasing concern over environmental issues, I felt there were surely opportunities to develop this area of business, and there were several successful environmental businesses and consultancies which provided models. Early in 1997 we decided to recruit someone to help develop our environmental business and appointed Dr Alan Fletcher, an experienced environmental consultant. At the same time, our non-executive director Dennis Stocks suggested that we should look at a small company based at Salford Quays, near Manchester, providing consultancy services to the water industry. He recommended that Rayna Dean, a corporate financial adviser with whom he had worked in the past, might help in making an approach to the company's owners.

Pipeline Developments Ltd (PDL) had been founded by Professor Phil Marshall, an engineer from the University of Salford, who had seen an opening in advising water companies on water distribution. The company undertook research and testing of pipeline materials and advised on water distribution networks and leak detection. With his energetic wife, Jackie, who looked after the administration, Phil had built up a successful business with a turnover of over £1 million pa. However, Phil and Jackie were planning to retire within a few years and were looking for a safe home for the company they had created. In the car on the way to my first visit to the Marshalls, Rayna told me a little about them and warned me that their two dogs came with them to work in their attractive, largely open-plan premises at Salford Quays. After being greeted by bounding dogs and being plied with huge sandwiches for lunch, we began our discussions. I explained why LGC might be interested in acquiring PDL; a combination of PDL's skills in water distribution, materials analysis and modelling with LGC's in water analysis and contaminated land would create a strong and credible contractor for the water industry in the UK and overseas.

During this and subsequent meetings we developed a mutual respect. In selling their company, Phil and Jackie obviously wanted to achieve a fair price, but they were equally concerned about the future of their staff and the business they had created. They liked what they heard about and saw of LGC and they identified with the culture I was trying to create. However, I was worried whether their business would continue to be successful without the dominant presence of the founders, particularly since it depended quite heavily on a relationship with one water utility company, North West Water. We eventually achieved an agreement whereby Phil and Jackie would continue to work for PDL for a couple of years and that part of the consideration for the sale would be an 'earn-out', payments geared to the profitability of the company over this two-year period. They would also help identify, appoint and train a new managing director who could run the company once they had left.

'Roses', the code name by which we called our project to acquire PDL, went smoothly, despite some last minute nerves on the part of the Marshalls. Rayna Dean helped with the financial due diligence and Alan Fletcher, who had just joined LGC, helped on the technical side, and we used a Manchester-based lawyer. I was keen to be sure that post-acquisition management arrangements were clear (which prompted the last-minute nerves) and, once the acquisition was announced in January 1998, I chaired the PDL board myself. I enjoyed visiting Salford Quays, an attractive redevelopment of land surrounding the Manchester Ship Canal, and relished the mixed atmosphere of past glories and new building, including The Lowry arts centre, which heralded the new millennium. Phil and Jackie Marshall were always hospitable (on a couple of occasions I stayed with them in their modern house a few minutes' walk from PDL's modern industrial unit) and they were very positive about being part of LGC.

As we proceeded with our acquisition of PDL, we were pursuing another concept, also ultimately involving expansion in the Northwest. During our discussions of strategy, we had spent some time analysing how the role of the Government Chemist might develop within our newly privatised organisation. A conclusion of the government's Technology Foresight inquiry, announced in the 1993 White Paper '*Realising our Potential*' was that analytical science in the UK was 'lagging behind', and that there needed to be concerted action by academics, industrialists, suppliers and other key players to invigorate analytical science and to spur the development and application of new techniques and systems. Dr Peter Lyne, who had joined LGC from BP, was tasked with building up relationships with the analytical science community, The Royal Society of Chemistry and the DTI, with a view to establishing partnerships to investigate new areas of analytical technology.

In parallel with these developments, we were exploring the concept of taking on 'outsourcing' work for industrial organisations. Outsourcing routine services, such as cleaning and catering, was commonplace, but there was a steady trend, in both the private and public sectors, towards outsourcing more sophisticated services. In relation to the public sector, LGC had begun to benefit from the 'market testing' policies introduced by the Conservative government (although we had also lost some work) and were anxious to find out what approach would be taken by the new Labour government elected in 1997. We needn't have worried. New Labour approached the contracting out of services with as much determination as the previous government and we soon appreciated that opportunities would open up for us in the public sector. However, we wanted to reduce our heavy reliance on public sector work and started investigating what opportunities there were to take over analytical services from companies which until recently had seen these as part of their 'core' activities. Our success in winning geochemical analysis work for BP and transferring staff and equipment from BP to LGC provided a model which we could explore with other companies who might consider outsourcing their analytical services.

I felt we should target the Northwest, for the simple reason that the region around Manchester and Liverpool and into Cheshire included a large number of chemical and pharmaceutical companies of all sizes which were potential customers for outsourcing. Our main laboratories in Teddington were well located for winning work outsourced from government, but were not ideally situated for close interactions with industry. A branch in the Northwest would give LGC credibility as the 'national centre' that we claimed to be. It transpired that there was a group of managers of analytical departments in the region, including those from ICI at Runcorn and Shell at Thornton, who had formed a 'club' for exchanging experiences. This seemed an obvious place for me to start.

The timing of my first approach, which was to the manager of analytical services at ICI's Runcorn Centre, could not have been more fortunate. ICI were going through massive changes and reorganising their business into more autonomous business units. The analytical services at Runcorn, which had already been substantially reduced in size, did not fit logically within a single business unit since they provided services across a range of ICI's business. Moving ICI's analytical services to LGC could actually assist with the reorganisation. A meeting with the ICI's Director of Research and Technology, Dr John Beacham, was arranged.

When Ray Ah-Sun and I entered Dr Beacham's office, armed with a carefully prepared presentation, we had no idea what sort of reception to expect. After I had explained about LGC and presented the concept of a centre of excellence for analytical science in the Northwest, we had a fascinating and open discussion. John immediately understood what we were trying to create and was encouraging, asking us to write with our proposals which he would discuss with colleagues. When we met again in London in a pub off Horse Guards Parade, John gave us further positive signals. We agreed that the project would be given the codename 'Dragoon' (there were pictures of dragoon guards on the wall of the bar!) and we would enter into serious confidential discussions.

ICI was not our only target in the Northwest. Shell had recently invested in new laboratories at its research centre at Thornton, adjacent to the massive Stanlow oil refinery, south of the Mersey estuary, near Ellesmere Port. The impressive laboratory blocks included one devoted to analytical science. If we could achieve an outsourcing arrangement with Shell, perhaps we could transfer ICI's analytical unit at Runcorn to this laboratory, thus making substantial savings in the high fixed costs involved in running laboratories. Before joining LGC, Ray Ah-Sun had worked for many years for Shell and understood their culture and decision-making processes.

Our early discussions with Shell seemed to go well. Like ICI, the company was undergoing some business changes, although not of such a fundamental nature. The outsourcing concept that we put forward seemed to strike a chord, but Shell would not make a move without consulting all the managers involved. Shell had a standard process to assess all new projects which lasted exactly 90 days. Ray and I found ourselves in meetings involving large numbers of people sitting on chairs arranged in a circle (sharing and non-confrontational) and 'brainstorming'. I was reminded of the 'case conferences' that Jacquie and I had endured in relation to our profoundly disabled daughter Helen, where everyone, including people we had never met and who had never met Helen, had an opinion to express, but no action was taken. There were times when I found it difficult to remain patient with Shell's processes, but Ray played along with the system (including writing his thoughts on yellow sticky labels for posting on a white board!) as best he could. I visited Shell's headquarters in The Hague and met their legal counsel and there were countless other meetings all of a surprisingly open nature. However, our discussions with Shell never really developed the momentum to lead to a deal and, in the end, we had to abandon them and take the risk of going it alone with ICI in the hope that other outsourcing business would materialise.

In July 1998, over a year after my first approach to ICI, it looked as if we would reach agreement on the terms of the transfer to LGC of ICI's analytical services. Finding an able manager to take on the current business but, more important, to develop other outsourcing opportunities, would be crucial to the success of the enterprise. I tentatively approached John Mason, with whom I had worked over many years and who was then in a managerial post in Teddington. He and his young family were settled in the Teddington area (his daughters used our staff nursery) and I wasn't sure how they would react to a move. I was delighted when he agreed to move to Cheshire to take charge of building up a business based on the core of ICI's analytical team, now reduced to just over 20 experienced people under the leadership of Steve Fletcher who, it was agreed, would not transfer to LGC. John was involved in the final negotiations which were greatly facilitated by Steve (who several years later actually joined LGC in a different capacity) and centred on a guarantee of work from ICI for 3 years and the always thorny issues of terms of employment and pensions. The deal we struck involved LGC acquiring the business assets and taking on its liabilities for a nominal £1 and, in October 1998, LGC's presence in the Northwest, a combination of Pipeline Developments Ltd and the Runcorn laboratories, gave us the credibility to approach new outsourcing customers.

Although our presence in the Northwest was primarily to develop our private sector business, it also linked with our plans to strengthen our position as the 'national centre' for analytical science. The privatisation agreements included a 'framework contract' with DTI under which support for the 'National Measurement System' (NMS) in relation to developing analytical standards was contracted to LGC. The layman usually takes measurement science for granted. We assume that a kilogram is a kilogram whatever weighing scales are used, and that a metre is the same distance in Japan as it is in France. In fact, for centuries there have been systems of standards for weights and measures, allowing rules and weighing scales to be calibrated. In 1875 there was a development of international significance: 17 countries signed The Convention of the Metre (Convention du Mètre), a treaty that created the International Bureau of Weights and Measures (BIPM), an inter-governmental organisation overseen by the International Committee for Weights and Measures (CIPM). Until the Second World War, the BIPM was mainly concerned with measurements of time, weight, length, and electricity and in developing standards for 'new' areas, such as radioactivity. However, the post-war period saw a huge increase in the need for complex measurements relating to, for example, food safety and quality, the environment, and health. Many of these – from trace measurements of heavy metals in water, to cholesterol levels in blood – are chemical or biological measurements for which developing a system of international standards is not straightforward. Whereas the public can be sure that a kilogram of rice is the same quantity whether purchased in Berlin or Baltimore (the scales are calibrated by standards which should ultimately trace back to the international kilogram held in a vault at the BIPM in Paris), a clinical measurement can often vary according to which laboratory the sample is sent to. In extreme cases, the treatment a patient receives can depend on the laboratory undertaking the diagnostic measurement. Measurement science, though not perhaps the most exciting or glamorous area of science, is crucially important to society, underpinning commercial transactions and international treaties. DTI contracted to LGC to take the lead for the UK in developing chemical and biochemical standards and we represented the UK on various international bodies.

DTI also contracted to LGC the work necessary for me to carry out my role as the Government Chemist. I took my responsibilities seriously and, with my colleagues, worked conscientiously to ensure that I fulfilled the functions which had been redefined under the privatisation agreements. The core of the work of the Government Chemist remained the statutory role as a referee analyst, a role which dated back to the nineteenth century. Under various Acts, if a substance (such as food suspected of being wrongly labelled or adulterated) was potentially going to be used as evidence in a prosecution, three samples would be taken for analysis – one for the enforcement body (usually Trading Standards), one for the trader to have analysed, and the third to be retained for the Government Chemist, should a dispute over the analysis arise subsequently between the enforcement body and the trader. In most cases, disputes were resolved before coming to court, thus saving public resources, but some complex cases reached court and LGC staff were called as expert witnesses. While the Laboratory was still an Agency, we had been involved in a high-profile case about pasta labelled as being made, as it should be, from durum (hard) wheat. Following investigations by Trading Standards, a major supermarket chain was to be prosecuted for selling pasta containing soft wheat, when it was labelled as containing 100% durum wheat. The trader disputed the analytical findings and a reference sample was sent to the Government Chemist. Fortunately, we were well prepared for this, as we had been aware for some time of possible fraud in the production of pasta. We developed three independent and highly sophisticated analytical methods and concluded that the 'durum wheat' pasta had been adulterated with a proportion of soft wheat. The case went to court and our expert was in the witness box for many hours. On the basis of our robust and detailed evidence, the trader was found guilty.

In the nineteenth century, disputes arose over alcoholic strength, the dilution of milk, and authenticity of food products. We continued to be involved in such cases, such as the strength of 'alcopops', the authenticity of a particular whisky or the amount of meat in a meat pie. In one such case, the Government Chemist's analysis of fish fingers confirmed that the white fish content, which had been declared as being 65%, was in fact considerably lower than what was stated on the label, and a successful prosecution was brought. However, not surprisingly, cases increasingly involved genetically modified foods and, in particular, GM soya, which was sometimes found in foodstuffs labelled as 'organic'. In order to be prepared for difficult cases, we had a small R&D programme aimed at validating new methods for the measurement of, for example, aflotoxins or trace amounts of organo-mercury compounds. Part of the role of the Government Chemist was being aware of issues which could potentially lead to trade or consumer protection disputes.

Each year I would write to the Secretary of State for Trade and Industry and report on the number of samples (mostly foodstuffs) sent to the Government Chemist for analysis and the nature of the dispute. I also highlighted policy areas where chemical analysis was relevant, such as regulation of the chemicals industry, forensic science and food safety. Mostly, I received an acknowledgement from the minister of the work carried out by the Laboratory over the previous year, but in 1998 I was surprised to receive a fulsome letter from the then Secretary of State, the Rt Hon Peter Mandelson (in response to the report which I had submitted to his predecessor, the Rt Hon Margaret Beckett); he said that he was 'intrigued to learn about the unique role of the Government Chemist and of the crucial and wide ranging work being carried out at LGC for Government and for industry'. Alas, he was soon to resign from DTI, and the following year I was writing to yet another Secretary of State, Stephen Byers, and a couple of years later, to Patricia Hewitt. The changes at the top of DTI no longer affected LGC directly, but the inevitable hiatus with each change meant that it was difficult for the Government Chemist to offer advice. It was not until the appointment of Lord (David) Sainsbury as Science Minister, that LGC in its privatised state registered again with government in any significant way.

However, partly because of the Government Chemist position, we felt that it was our role to promote the importance of chemical measurement to senior people in industry, to politicians and to senior civil servants. To this end I regularly issued invitations for visits to LGC's laboratories at Teddington. The format of the visits was usually the same: arrival at

10.30 with introduction and a short presentation from me over coffee, visit to three laboratories likely to be of interest to the visitor, and general discussion over a buffet lunch before departure. I reckoned that most visitors simply gained an impression of the organisation and only retained a few points, but it was important that our enthusiasm came across, and I often rehearsed staff to ensure that their presentations highlighted just a few essential messages we wanted to convey. Whenever possible I tried to involve younger staff in the laboratory tours to give them experience of presenting, often to non-technical visitors. The slow but constant stream of senior people coming to LGC at Teddington (I invited members of parliament, government and opposition officials, industry representatives, senior trades union officials, academics, embassy officials, and so on) built awareness of our positive, dynamic and successful organisation, and this paid dividends in the future.

This was the format for a visit by Toby Jessel, the rather eccentric Conservative Member of Parliament for Twickenham until his defeat in the 1997 election. He was clearly impressed by his visit, in particular his tour of our drugs analysis laboratory where he saw a particularly large seizure of cocaine, as well as heroin and cannabis awaiting analysis. He wanted to be photographed with the seizures and then to issue a press release declaring how proud he was that LGC 'did work important to every man, woman and child in the country', and that the organisation was based in his constituency. I had tactfully to explain that we were not keen to advertise the fact that at that time we had cocaine worth many millions of pounds in our laboratory. I also invited his successor, Vince Cable, to visit several times and on one occasion he brought with him Charles Kennedy, then leader of the Liberal Democrats, and their London Mayoral candidate, Susan Kramer. On this occasion Charles Kennedy gave a television interview in our DNA laboratory. When Lord Sainsbury, the Science Minister, visited he provided a sample of saliva at the beginning of his visit to our DNA and other laboratories at Teddington and we then provided him with a genetic scan at the end of his visit. (We had cleared in advance that he was willing to take part in this trial.) He was impressed with the speed of the measurement, and subsequently quoted this as a powerful demonstration of the rapid DNA technology we had developed.

However, it was not just senior people and politicians that I felt it important to cultivate. There was a desperate need to raise positive awareness of science among the general public, and campaigns to this end were being led by the Royal Society and other eminent bodies. It seemed to me that LGC should devote effort to helping to promote the importance of science in general, and analytical science in particular. As part of our 'national centre' function we employed a very small team who worked with schools and universities providing curriculum material on analytical science. We sponsored an annual schools' competition and we hosted numerous school visits to our splendid Teddington facilities. We encouraged work experience placements for school and college students and ran frequent practical training courses for teachers and lecturers. I was particularly keen that we should hold open days on which members of the general public, particularly those who lived in South West London, could come and visit our laboratories and see demonstrations of our work and ask questions of our staff. Open days, by now held at Runcorn as well as Teddington, also provided the opportunity for staff to bring their friends and families to see where they worked. LGC was in a strong position to present science in a very positive manner; our varied work, from forensic investigations to checking the safety of toys, was of great interest to members of the public and they could immediately appreciate its importance. An area of our work which always fascinated our visitors, though slightly strange to find within an analytical laboratory, was Questioned Documents. Our work examining handwriting dated back to the introduction of the old age pension in 1909 when the Laboratory was called in to examine birth certificates which were suspected of having been altered to increase the age of the person claiming the new benefit. LGC was still involved in cases of benefit fraud and worked on many high-profile cases. For example, in 1987 we had been called upon to certify the suicide note left in Spandau Prison by Rudolf Hess. In this and many other areas it was rewarding to see the enthusiasm of staff in presenting their work to spellbound visitors. It was also good to be questioned by members of the public and to engage in discussion of, for example, genetically modified food. Of course these initiatives were quite expensive and sometimes disrupted the work of the company, but I believed strongly that they were essential to encourage young people to pursue scientific careers and to help address some of the misunderstandings about science among the public.

In order to support our case for the importance of chemical measurement we commissioned a piece of market research which we published in 1998 which involved interviews with senior decision-makers in industry, such as technical directors, to probe the issues surrounding recruitment of analysts, organisation of the analytical function, investment in analysis and outsourcing of analytical work. It appeared that analysis was often seen as very important, key to research or quality control, but that analysts themselves were regarded in a less positive light. In conjunction with economists at DTI, we also commissioned some economic research, from Manchester Business School, to advise on possible approaches to the difficult problem of assigning value to the analytical component of activities and quantifying the economic benefit of analytical measurements. Some earlier work had already shown that there were some 20,000 analytical laboratories in the UK, employing around 200,000 people. The size of the 'sector' (which in fact was a small part of many other sectors such as pharmaceuticals, chemicals/petroleum, food/drink) often surprised even those involved in science policy.

There was another purpose in highlighting the economic aspects of analytical science. Politicians now accept that technological innovation has an important role in the economy, generating new products and opening up new markets. Recent years have seen a transformation in the way innovative scientific work carried out in UK universities has led to new business opportunities, and numerous reports have highlighted the importance of technical innovation. High-tech spin-out companies are now encouraged and fostered. However, it is not always understood by those who have had little contact with science-based industries that business success does not depend simply on novel science; other steps including product development, quality assurance, and marketing are crucially important. The UK has an excellent record in scientific and technical innovation, but has been far less successful at exploiting innovations in the market place. There are numerous examples of British inventions not being exploited successfully by British companies. I believe this is partly the result of a snobbery, now fortunately less evident, which regarded pure science as admirable but applied science as being too close to 'trade'. In relation to analytical science, an analytical method may be based on an innovative scientific procedure, but using this method in practical situations requires many other disciplines. The investment in the successful exploitation of the new method cannot be simply in the initial research but must also be in the long grind of development and validation.

The experience we were gaining in our interactions with industry and government reinforced the need for better standards for the analytical sector. For many years LGC had produced a small number of 'reference materials' which were supplied to laboratories to allow analytical chemists to check their measurements against the reference material standard. In some ways reference materials can be regarded as the chemical equivalent of calibrated weights. However, in chemical analysis it is frequently necessary to extract the chemical you want to measure from the material in which it is found. Unlike with a physical measurement, when weighing stone, for example, is no different from weighing sand, chemical measurements depend on the chemical nature of the material under investigation and whether the analyte, the substance to be measured, is a pure substance or, as is often the case, is embedded in a matrix. It is sometimes necessary to measure the concentration of, for example, pure pesticide, but more frequently the measurement requires first extracting the analyte (the pesticide) from a matrix, for example a fruit which has been sprayed. Whereas in physical measurement of weight it is possible to use one set of calibrated standards for measuring the weight of diamonds or rubies, in chemical analysis different sets of 'chemical weights' are necessary for different types of chemicals. The 'chemical weights', or rather 'chemical reference materials', are sometimes pure substances (such as pure silver as a comparison for measuring the purity of jewellery) but it is frequently more useful to have a reference material consisting of an analyte contained within a matrix, such as alcohol in wine, lead in petrol, or even cannabis in freeze-dried urine. A laboratory analyst tasked with measuring alcohol content makes a measurement in the sample under investigation and then carries out a similar measurement on a reference standard. The result for the test sample can be compared with the result for the alcohol/wine reference material which contains an amount of alcohol (which is on the analytical certificate) predetermined by more sophisticated means in a standards laboratory such as LGC. Some alcohol standards are simply cans of wine or beer which are not themselves particularly expensive but which have been carefully prepared in batches and analysed with great precision to provide a very accurate benchmark for other laboratories to use. Other reference materials, such as pesticides in apple leaves, or pharmaceuticals containing known amounts of impurities, are uniform powders stored in small brown bottles. Reference materials may degrade with time, and so keeping stocks of up-to-date materials may involve the regular production and certification of new batches.

The huge expansion of international trade in the second half of the last century and the development of international regulations covering, for example, food, consumer goods, toys and the environment, required analysts to ensure that their measurements were equivalent to those made elsewhere. Reference materials are one of the ways used to demonstrate that this is the case and the demand for these steadily increased. There were several organisations that produced reference materials, such as the US National Institute for Science and Technology (NIST) and the Community Bureau of Reference (BCR), a European research programme established in 1973 to develop reference materials collaboratively across Europe, and there were some private suppliers too. LGC manufactured and certified a small range of reference materials and had established a small office to provide advice on reference materials from other producers and to sell them. Although we produced catalogues and had databases, our operations, which had been run for many years more or less as a public service, were rather amateurish from a commercial point of view.

We were well aware that a much more successful reference materials distribution business called Promochem had been established in Germany and was expanding into the UK and other European countries. Promochem did not manufacture or assign values to reference materials, but simply acted as a highly professional distribution organisation for materials coming from all parts of the world. The company had been founded by an Englishman, Ken Jenkins, living in Germany, who spotted the need, particularly in the aftermath of the dreadful Seveso accident, for reference standards for environmental measurements of pesticides. With his German partner, Tilo Karrer, he built up a successful business supplying these standards from their unit in Wesel, a small city in

North Rhine-Westphalia. Later, Ken was joined by his brother, David Jenkins, who established an office in the UK. The possibility of merging LGC's manufacturing and advisory business with Promochem's highly professional distribution business was very attractive; it would certainly accelerate our efforts to establish ourselves as the pre-eminent standard-setting company.

After some low-key discussions, Ray Ah-Sun and I invited Ken and David to Teddington where we proposed a merger of our businesses. Partly because they were beginning to think of retirement, the brothers were receptive to the idea and, after further discussions at Wesel of valuations and how we would join forces, and with the agreement of LGC's board, I asked David Haggett, Eversheds' managing partner, who had become a good friend, to help draft the offer letter. One morning, sitting at the dining room table in our house in Abingdon, David drafted a beautifully elegant and persuasive letter which I duly sent to the three main shareholders. The two brothers accepted our offer and we shook hands on the deal. However, unbeknown to any of us, Tilo, who his co-owners had assumed would fall into line with them, had approached a bank in Wesel and had arranged to borrow sufficient money to match LGC's offer. He exercised his pre-emption rights to buy the business outright.

To say that I was disappointed would be an understatement. We had been working long hours and weekends on a deal which could have been another major step towards transforming LGC. However, I wrote a letter to Tilo congratulating him on buying the business and suggesting that we might keep in touch in the future, and spent the break for Christmas 1998 thinking about what our next move should be. When Ray returned in the New Year we discussed a 'plan B' in which LGC would open offices to compete directly with Promochem. This expansion of our reference standards business (which we called Project Fenix – for obvious reasons, but with altered spelling) would take longer but would cost less. We managed to recruit a couple of disillusioned Promochem managers and some junior staff. In 1999 we formed companies in France and Sweden and in 2000 we opened a sales office in Spain.

Linking our reference materials business with our work in support of international standards was an essential part of my vision for the company and became central to the marketing strategy for the business. On joining LGC I had been asked to be a UK representative on the General Assembly of Eurolab, a European federation of national associations of measurement, testing and analytical laboratories, and I attended meetings twice a year. I subsequently was elected to Eurolab's Board of Administrators. LGC also helped to found, and contributed strongly to, Eurachem, another pan-European grouping, which met to consider the more technical aspects of traceability of chemical measurements. Meetings of these organisations were not always very stimulating, but I firmly believed that the UK should have a strong voice in an expanding Europe, and standards-setting and testing were essential to creating a fully functional single European market. As someone who believes strongly in the benefits – political, trade and cultural – of the European Union, I was often frustrated by the attitude of the British towards Europe. If we continued to appear reluctant to participate, there was a danger that the UK would lose influence in fields where we were strong. I felt that the UK was in a particularly good position, not least because of our language, to ensure that regulation of measurement and testing was proportionate and based on sound science, and that we could influence the development of measurement infrastructure in the accessioning countries. I noted that the French and German governments provided financial support and were fully engaged in facilitating the infrastructure in support of trading standards.

Through my involvement in Eurolab I met directors of all the major public sector measurement and testing establishments in Europe and a wide range of industrialists. Among the many people I got to know was Claes Bankvall, the director of SP, the Swedish National Testing Institute. I approached him about LGC's plans to set up a distribution company in Sweden and to my delight he agreed to rent us space (an office and store) within SP's impressive facilities in the small town of Borås, about an hour's drive from Gothenburg. To be co-located in the Swedish centre for measurement would reinforce our strategy of building a brand around 'setting standards in analytical science'.

Our reference standards business was given a huge boost by two major deals we struck with US suppliers. The first was an agreement with the US Pharmacopeia (USP) to become a distributor in Europe, alongside Promochem, of their pharmaceutical reference materials, used by pharmaceutical companies all over the world. The second was an exclusive arrangement with the American Type Culture Collection (ATCC), a US federal, independent not-for-profit organisation, which managed the largest collection in the world of biological materials for research, including cell lines, molecular genomics tools, micro-organisms and bioproducts. We invited ATCC's director, Dr Ray Cypess and his wife, to visit our Teddington laboratories and, on a sunny day at the end of July 1999, after discussions at Teddington, Ray Ah-Sun and I took our guests for an early dinner at The Mitre Hotel opposite Hampton Court overlooking the Thames. Typical of his attention to detail, Ray had found out that it was Dr Cypess's birthday and had arranged with Dr Cypess's PA for a card to be sent, signed by his staff. This was presented along with a birthday cake prepared by the restaurant at the end of our most enjoyable and convivial meal. However, underlying this bonhomie was a serious mutual understanding that ATCC and LGC had much in common and that an alliance between the two organisations could bring about a powerful combination of ATCC's biological resources and LGC's scientific and business acumen. Although our distribution network was only just being established, Dr Cypess was positive about a joint working arrangement with LGC under which LGC would distribute ATCC materials to research scientists outside the US. By April the following year we had the staff recruited and the necessary cryogenic storage facilities in place at Teddington to allow us to sign a contract for the exclusive supply of ATCC materials in Europe.

Project Fenix, our plan to develop a Europe-wide reference materials business, was very exciting and proving successful. However, although our business was expanding quite rapidly, the path we were pursuing of organic growth would take time. Moreover, although we were having an impact on Promochem's business, they were continuing to do well. During the summer of 2000 I suggested to Ray that we might make a second attempt to merge with Promochem. I instinctively sensed that there had been cultural and language issues in our previous discussions which might have made Tilo Karrer, now Promochem's sole shareholder, suspicious, and felt that the first approach should be made by an intermediary, with a perfect command of German, rather than directly by me. Our non-executive director, Dennis Stocks, had previously worked closely with Uwe de Buhr, a very successful German businessman who had recently retired. I briefed Uwe on the background to LGC's relationship with Promochem and he arranged to meet Tilo to sound out his willingness to re-open discussions. The response Uwe received was cautious, but both sides promised that our discussions should be absolutely secret; we were aware that any leak would have a devastating effect on our staff and businesses.

With Uwe acting as cultural attaché, Tilo, Ray Ah-Sun and I met at the Ibis Hotel, Luton airport at the end of September 2000. The atmosphere was initially tense, but we all recognised the huge business advantages in combining LGC's scientific expertise and growing reference materials business with Promochem's well-established business and market experience. Thanks to gentle humour injected by Uwe, the discussion became more relaxed and we began to consider how the two businesses might fit together. By the end, it was agreed that Tilo would consult his adviser and indicate what price he expected for the business.

Things moved rapidly. A meeting was arranged with Tilo and his adviser, this time at Dusseldorf airport, and I returned to Dusseldorf at the end of November for further negotiations. I was back in Dusseldorf again 10 days later for final price negotiations. It was a long meeting during which Uwe and I left Tilo and his adviser to discuss things on their own for quite long periods but, just in time for my late flight back to Heathrow, we had agreed the main terms. As always, the actual sale and purchase agreement and all the other legal agreements associated with the transaction took some time to hammer out, but finally, on 6 June 2001, LGC acquired all the shares in Promochem GmbH (the German holding company) and Promochem's separate companies in France, Spain and England, and Promochem's shareholdings in its companies in Sweden, Poland and India. We kept the deal secret until Tilo, Ray and I could visit our sites in Wesel and Strasbourg and then in the UK to deliver the news directly to staff.

So, nearly three years after our initial approach to Promochem, we had achieved the merger which would form the foundation of a highly successful division of LGC, initially branded as 'LGC Promochem' but ultimately renamed 'LGC Standards'. It was a hugely important and transformational move, and I felt triumphant to have pulled it off. Not that the marriage was without some initial problems; although we had developed detailed plans for the integration of our two businesses, not surprisingly there were conflicts to resolve in units which had previously been bitter rivals, and inevitably some people left the company, not all voluntarily. However, the general manager I had recruited specifically to run the combined businesses, Liz Bewick (subsequently Liz Jordain), worked tirelessly with Ray, Uwe and others to create a new organisation, and within a year or so, the business was on the path of strong growth, which has continued ever since.

During the three-year period of the emergence of our new reference standards business, we were active on a large number of other projects. It was a period of great creativity, analysing our strength and technological expertise and matching them with a wide range of market opportunities. Ray Ah-Sun and I, separately and together, spent a lot of time visiting companies, small and large, pursuing business ideas and prospects, some of which were to transform our business. Of course, not all our initiatives were successful. I reckoned that if more than one in every ten of our new ideas developed into new business activities we were doing well, but we probably exceeded this target.

Some new ventures took off but, as one would expect, some never completely realised their potential. Although PDL was proving successful at winning new business, our efforts to develop other environmental business were struggling. In particular, we had jointly formed a company, Pure Risk Management Ltd, with academic and legal partners, to carry out environmental assessments. The company was based in a Victorian house adjacent to LGC's laboratories at Teddington and, like the rest of our environmental business, had a business plan which was extremely optimistic. Unfortunately, month after month our environmental business fell short of its targets and I concluded that we should be decisive and abandon our efforts in this field. Alan Fletcher, who had been with us for only a couple of years, fully understood the position and quickly found another post, and we parted company in a friendly manner, leaving us to wind up Pure Risk Management, and learn from the experience of a start-up that had never got off the blocks. My decision to exit from a business which had not been going long was not easy, but it is usually best to acknowledge a mistake and to move on as quickly as possible, rather than allowing time to pass, and losses to accumulate, in the hope that things will eventually look up.

We looked at a string of possible acquisitions, some of which got to quite an advanced stage. Among the first that we considered was a profitable food testing business called Aspen and James. Ray Ah-Sun was persuaded that this could complement our own food analytical capabilities which were focused on public sector work. I was less sure; I was not convinced that it was right for LGC, in that this type of testing might take us too far 'down market' from our strategy position at the 'high end' of analytical services. Negotiations had gone quite a long way before we decided to withdraw from the process. In the event, Aspen and James was sold in 1998 to Mid Kent Holdings and continued as Eclipse Scientific.

I was much keener on another opportunity which arose a little later. In June 1999 I telephoned, and subsequently met, John Patterson, Executive Vice President of Product Strategy and Licensing of the recently merged pharmaceutical giant, AstraZeneca. I asked him whether he would be prepared to sell Cellmark, a small genetic testing company that had been set up by ICI and had transferred to Zeneca under ICI's de-merger arrangements. I figured that Cellmark would be 'non-core' to AstraZeneca and that they might be pleased to find it a new home. LGC would be able to combine the unit with our rapidly expanding life science activities which were led by Paul Debenham, who had actually been the scientific director of Cellmark before joining University Diagnostics. It would create a formidable force. The response I got from John Patterson was positive and he tasked his deputy Roger Lloyd with following up the proposal. I was hoping the deal would be done in the same way as we had acquired ICI Runcorn analytical services. However, Roger went about it in a more structured way, preparing an information memorandum which was circulated to other parties as well as LGC. Nevertheless, I developed a good relationship with Roger and LGC submitted a reasonable cash bid. Unbeknown to us, however, a small US company called Orchid were also interested in Cellmark as the nucleus for expanding into Europe. It later transpired that their bid was in shares and a technology exchange. Early in 2000 AstraZeneca told us that they were selling Cellmark to Orchid. The fact that Orchid's share value subsequently plummeted and that the technology exchange proved of little value, leaving AZ with little to show for the transaction, was no comfort. I was disappointed at having identified this opportunity, nurtured it, but not secured it.

The acquisition of Promochem and our effort to acquire Cellmark had taken time, but these projects were just two amongst many. Other potential acquisitions we investigated included AEA's analytical services at Harwell and ICI's analytical services in the Northeast at Wilton. However, looking for transformational deals was not just about acquisitions. Our core business was growing fast and we were winning contracts from all parts of government and, increasingly, from the private sector.

A major opportunity arose at the end of 1997 when the Veterinary Medicines Directorate, an agency of the Ministry of Agriculture, Fisheries and Food (MAFF) decided to market test the analytical work associated with their statutory food surveillance programme which was at the time carried out within MAFF's own Veterinary Laboratories Agency at Weybridge. This was a very large programme and, although LGC had some experience of detecting minute quantities of drug and pesticide residues in foodstuffs, we had never done work like this on such a large scale, against tight deadlines. Ian Lumley, who was in charge of our food business, approached the preparation of our tender submission in a highly professional manner. We investigated alternative analytical technologies and considered every detail of the complex logistics of receiving large numbers of samples from all over the country. Our relatively new Laboratory Information Managements System (LIMS) which was proving so powerful in our DNA laboratory would be adapted for this new contract. The night before the deadline for submitting our proposal we were still writing part of it and I joined the small team to help assemble and bind the huge document which was delivered by hand the following morning.

We were visited by senior VMD staff and their advisers who audited our facilities and I led a small team to VMD to present our proposal to the evaluation panel. We had rehearsed our presentation over and over again. I gave a short introduction, reinforcing our company's commitment to the work, and Ian Lumley and his colleagues gave excellent technical presentations. The IT system which Surrinder Johal (who had helped set up our DNA forensics laboratory) outlined clearly impressed the assessors. We felt that our proposal had been well received, but for weeks we heard nothing. Initially all our enquiries were brushed aside, but eventually we started to receive some slightly positive feedback. We heard later that there had been major upset within MAFF because their own agencies, VLA and CSL, were not being awarded the contract and that eventually it had been a ministerial decision to award it to LGC. The feeling of elation when we received the news that we had won the contract was tremendous. The contract was for up to five years and worth millions of pounds. Not only did it represent a major addition to our business, but it would enhance our position as a centre of excellence for such work. However, it rapidly dawned that we had less than six months to prepare the new laboratory and develop the necessary methods to undertake this major programme.

The first year of the contract which began in January 1999 was not easy. Although everyone worked hard to deliver the work and to maintain good relations with our customer, we were unable to keep up with the influx of samples arriving for analysis. We had introduced some new screening methods, but many of the analytical methods which we had inherited from the Veterinary Laboratories Agency were old and labour intensive. Our increasing backlog became embarrassingly visible as we had to install large portable freezers in our staff car park to store samples awaiting analysis. This set other scientists around the laboratory thinking about how the situation could be resolved (ideally before all car parking spaces had disappeared!). We had recently acquired a new type of instrument, a tandem mass spectrometer for high accuracy analysis in connection with our standards work. Tim Catterick, who led the team involved in this work, realised that the technique could also be used for veterinary drug residue analysis. By combining screening, identification and quantification in one single run, significant improvements in productivity and throughput could be achieved. Tim consequently 'donated' his instrument to the cause. New methods were validated as quickly as possible and the unsightly freezers, a very visible reminder that we were behind schedule, were eventually removed from the car park.

Tim Catterick's team did not entirely lose out; he was able to acquire a new instrument, several times more sensitive than the 9-month-old instrument he had released for the VMD programme, illustrating the pace of instrument development at this time. Instruments costing in the order of £250,000 could rapidly become obsolete for leading edge work. This episode also illustrated the advantage of having wide-ranging analytical R&D and service work at LGC and the importance of staff communication and collaboration across the laboratory. It marked the start of a significant further investment in tandem mass spectrometry for both research and high-end analytical services.

The veterinary residue surveillance work was part of a European Union-wide programme and the Food and Veterinary Office (FVO) of the European Commission was very suspicious of a programme to ensure the safety of European consumers being carried out by a private company. As part of their audit programme, the FVO sent a team to inspect our work. The auditors came from the network of public sector laboratories and made clear that they were unhappy about LGC, a private company, undertaking this work, although they were rather taken aback, and clearly impressed, by the advanced analytical methods we were using. Nevertheless, we were criticised for not completing our work within the required timescales. We threw resources at tackling the problem, kept our customer fully informed, and eventually we managed to get on top of the work, but not without financial consequences for the first year. Thankfully, the situation began to stabilise and we were able to introduce new and streamlined working methods and to recover some of our substantial investment. Recognising that some of the problems were administrative, I suggested that my very capable personal assistant, Pam Hancock, might join the team, now led by an able young scientist, John Points, in order to introduce more effective administrative systems. She contributed to changing our new veterinary medicines laboratory from being a focus of concern into a model of a well-managed facility which we were proud to show to visitors. VMD was delighted with the quality and responsiveness of our team and five years later, when the work was re-tendered, again against strong competition, we were awarded a second five-year contract.

A rather different business opportunity arose in the area of genetic testing. Paul Debenham had for some time been interested in pharmacogenetics, the way people's different genetic make-up gives rise to different responses to therapeutic drugs. Professor Roland Wolf, then at Dundee

University, had shown that a particular gene sequence, CYP2D6, could be used to predict how people metabolised common drugs. For example, up to 10% of people taking codeine for pain relief are unable to metabolise it and receive little benefit, and suffer the side effect of drowsiness, from the drug. (By coincidence, Paul himself had discovered that he was a poor codeine metaboliser.) Roland Wolf had patented the gene and Paul was interested in the possibility of sub-licensing rights to allow LGC to provide a pharmacogenetics testing service.

By chance I knew Bob Smailes who was the commercial manager at Dundee University and I invited him to visit LGC to discuss a sub-licence arrangement. With rather little experience in providing diagnostic services, LGC was not the obvious company to exploit this test but, after lengthy discussions with Dundee and the other bodies with patent ownership rights, we agreed sub-licensing arrangements. 'Personalised medicine' was a topic which had reached the popular press and this was an area of genetic testing where the benefits seemed uncontroversial. However, although we achieved some very useful publicity, the business grew less rapidly than we had hoped.

We also investigated another genetic test which had arisen from the study of Mormon family records at Salt Lake City. A company called Myriad had discovered genes (BRCA I and BRCA II) which are related to an inherited form of breast cancer particularly prevalent amongst Ashkenazi Jews. Myriad offered tests to families in the USA most likely to be affected by this inherited gene and, after some initial contacts, Paul Debenham and I visited Myriad to discuss a possible licence for LGC in Europe. The test was more controversial because the patent was disputed in Europe. Indeed, some European countries were maintaining that patenting genetic sequences should not be permitted. We had discussions with the Department of Health and a number of geneticists in the UK. Although we received some support in our efforts to set up a high quality genetic service, this initiative got mired in bureaucracy and showed us how difficult it would be to break into providing services to the NHS.

Although much of my effort was devoted to raising LGC's profile and developing new business, there were many changes that I wanted to make within the organisation. Bidding for, and winning, new work was very exciting, but once a contract had been signed, we had to ensure that we could gear up quickly to delivering it. New staff and new management arrangements were needed. LGC was beginning to change radically and we needed to articulate a revised and coherent strategy. In 1999, with the agreement of the board, I decided to attend a short course at INSEAD, the European business school to have time to think about different approaches to strategic business management. The course I went to at INSEAD was for 'owner directors' of businesses and consisted of two separate intensive weeks, one in June and the second in November. The standard of teaching, based on case studies, was very high and the small group was very interactive. It was fascinating to exchange experiences with other entrepreneurs who had set up and run a wide range of businesses. Above all, it provided an opportunity to stand back and analyse the challenges faced by LGC in relation to those in other businesses and to consider the leadership which would be required to sustain and accelerate LGC's growth.

Earlier in 1999 Adrian Wilson, our Finance Director who had loyally supported my management buy-out and had worked tirelessly to help establish the new company, retired and was replaced by Clive Hall, who joined us from Powergen where he was head of tax. Clive's remit at LGC was to introduce the financial disciplines and systems to cope with our growth and to help me develop a business plan which would set out our funding and investment requirements for the following few years. Clive set to work on a new corporate plan and gathered data and proposals from each of our operational divisions. As part of the process, the senior management team met for a couple of days at a hotel in the Midlands, a location significantly and strategically chosen to demonstrate the expansion of the company, then spread between our main Teddington operations and our burgeoning operations in the Northwest. At this conference we considered what targets we should set ourselves and what we would need to do to achieve them. Our conclusions formed the basis of a high-level plan which was to set ambitious goals for the company and guide our decision-making over the coming eventful years.

Chapter 5: *Bold plans*

A new vision for LGC – Managing change and the Pentagon programme – Staff share ownership – Genotyping sheep – Preventing a national catastrophe – Food safety and BSE

The corporate plan which we worked on during 1999 was to set our course for the next five years. The headline target for the plan was to increase turnover from £22m expected for 1999/2000 to £100m within 5 years, to be achieved through a combination of organic growth, 'new ventures' (such as forensic DNA profiling and the major contract we had won from VMD, which had required significant investment in new staff and facilities) and acquisitions. At the same time we aimed to improve our profitability from its current modest level to above 10% of sales. The plan set out a new 'vision' for the company which was 'To be an international business recognised for setting standards in analytical science and providing best value services, products and solutions'. (I always felt that 'solutions' was a bit of a cliché and we later dropped it.) The plan envisaged over 25% of sales from outside the UK, and sales to the private sector increasing to over 40% of total revenues. The plan would require major changes which were set out in a series of strategic objectives.

The plan was undoubtedly a bold statement of intent and when I presented it to staff, there were some who were cynical about whether the ambitious targets could be achieved. The high level targets were significant. Up until then, the company had depended to a large extent on UK public sector contracts. Partly to reduce this dependence and partly to gain access to markets with greater potential for profitable growth, I wanted to accelerate our efforts to increase the private sector component, and to press ahead with our expansion into other European countries and beyond. I felt it was important to provide a coherent and straightforward description of our strategy. A simple diagrammatic model was used to show how LGC intended to continue to address sophisticated analytical problems with advanced techniques, but that we would also expand into the larger markets for more routine analytical services by developing advanced high throughput methods. To keep things simple, I boiled the changes which would be necessary down to five strategic objectives: promoting our brand internationally; continuous improvement in our efficiency; investment in technology; focus on customer service; and the development of our staff. For the purposes of presentation, I arranged them as the five sides of a pentagon and 'The Pentagon Programme' was to become the main vehicle for changing the organisation over the coming years.

The Pentagon Programme brought together a series of imaginative initiatives, some of which were already under way, under the five strategic areas. For example, we had established several initiatives to promote a wider understanding within the company of the scientific context of our work, and these became part of the science and technology Pentagon objective. We invited speakers to give lunchtime lectures and all staff, including those from service departments, were free to attend. Speakers included Professor Hugh Pennington who talked about the causes of food poisoning, Professor Carol Sikora about cancer treatment, and Professor Stanley Prusiner about prion diseases (such as BSE). Our own scientific staff also gave some excellent talks about their work.

Another theme of the Pentagon Programme was focusing on customers. We had been working hard to improve our approach to customer care (from telephone answering to dealing with complaints) and had instituted training programmes and awareness-raising schemes. We expanded these and put them together under the Pentagon Programme umbrella, and introduced new initiatives on operational efficiency, the use of finance in decision-making, and so on. It was important to launch initiatives to change the focus of the organisation but I was wary of the danger of 'initiative fatigue' setting in. The Pentagon Programme linked the initiatives, creating a single programme for change. It aimed to provide clarity and reinforce a culture of common purpose.

The key area in our Pentagon Programme was staff development and I was convinced that this, more than anything else, would influence our success in achieving the objectives in our corporate plan. The company had already expanded during its early years; there were many new staff, although inevitably there had been a number of resignations and redundancies from areas which were less successful. By March 1999, just three years after the company had been launched, over 40% of our staff (now totalling 375, compared with 272 in 1996) had been with the company for less than three years. Over half of our staff were now aged under 35. We had managed to recruit some excellent people with managerial as well as technical skills, but we remained short of experienced managers. Inspired by my own recent excellent management course at INSEAD, I asked Peter Lyne to help me develop a management course targeted at middle managers who we felt had the potential to develop to take on new managerial roles.

Peter and I set about finding a business school which would provide us with high quality training tailored to our own particular staff needs. My phone call to London Business School was met rather snootily with the response that they would not consider dealing with an organisation with a turnover of less than £0.5 billion. My plan to achieve this figure through management development cut no ice! Cranfield proposed an interesting programme which, intriguingly, included using actors from the Royal Shakespeare Company in role play activities aimed at developing leadership skills. However, we felt that the best programme was offered by Ashridge Business School which had fully understood our brief and also appreciated that, at this stage in our development, we had little cash to spare and needed to squeeze the juice out of every pound we spent on training. In 2000, eighteen of our managers, including Peter Lyne, successfully completed a course which consisted of two separate weeks when they were exposed to fundamental concepts in marketing, finance, operational performance and working in teams. In the few weeks between the two residential weeks the participants, while back in their jobs, took part in projects and presented their findings to the whole management team. I interviewed individually all those who attended the course, both before and afterwards, and Peter Lyne and I kept in close contact with the excellent course tutors at Ashridge. The course was obviously expensive – over £4,000 for each participant – but it was a huge success, in terms of both the development of management skills and in motivating the participants, who kept in touch with one other afterwards, forming a cadre of highly motivated managers. We repeated the exercise, with only minor changes, the following year and several times after that, so that within a relatively short period a high proportion of our ablest staff were exposed to the

Ashridge experience. A side benefit of the programme was that managers met others from different departments and disciplines and different parts of the company, from our UK and other European branches, which helped spread awareness of the company's activities and break down barriers between, for example, scientific and administrative teams.

Although short courses and away days for managers may sometimes appear wasteful, in that they obviously cost money to organise and, perhaps more significantly, take staff from away from their important work, they are an essential way of gradually improving performance and, if necessary, changing aspects of the culture of an organisation. By introducing many new staff, LGC's rapid growth could have threatened the corporate identity and culture that I was trying to create. It was particularly important that staff should get a feel for the whole organisation and have an understanding of the company's overall objectives. In this context, the Pentagon Programme provided a focus for the changes we wanted to make, and regular informal soundings of staff, as well as more formal staff surveys, demonstrated that it was highly successful in influencing LGC's development.

Nurturing and developing up-and-coming managers was only part of the staff development challenge. Having agreed changes in terms and conditions which moved staff away from the civil service system, we introduced new performance management arrangements which included an element of performance-related pay. Reviews of our final salary pension scheme concluded that it would be an impossible financial burden to sustain this in the longer term, and regretfully we closed the scheme to new members and limited benefits to existing members, setting up an alternative but generous contribution scheme for new members. On a more positive note, we introduced a series of short management skills training courses for all levels within the organisation (which we later called ManSki) and set ourselves internal targets for training within the company which were well received. However, there were other less formal means of motivating staff. Shortly after the company's formation we held a Christmas dinner party for staff and their partners. As the company grew, we adopted a less formal format for regular staff parties, which were great fun and much enjoyed by all.

When we acquired University Diagnostics we discovered that the staff regularly got involved in fundraising activities for charity. We decided to introduce a similar charity programme throughout LGC, adopting UDL's charity – Jeans for Genes – as our first company-wide cause for which to raise money. LGC agreed to match any funds raised by staff through a range of individual initiatives, from sponsored cycle rides to cake sales. This also led to an annual summer fete, held on a large lawn in front of the Teddington laboratory, which had a remarkable variety of stalls and ended, much to the entertainment of all staff, with highly competitive three-legged or sack races among the executive management team. Another money-raising activity was 'foods from around the world' when our increasingly international and multi-cultured staff would prepare dishes from many different nations for their colleagues to sample. This also led to the preparation of a cookbook, sold in aid of the company charity. (Apart from providing some delicious recipes, this cookbook demonstrated how LGC had evolved from its civil service roots into a diverse company drawing on the skills of people from many different cultures, including from the countries where we had now set up operations.) Each year a small committee of staff selected a new charity to support, often with a connection to LGC's work, and we invited a speaker from the chosen charity to address staff. The charities we backed included the Anthony Nolan Trust, Médécins sans Frontières, Cancer Research UK, Water Aid, Sane and Alzheimer's Society. (Where a charity was not international, we asked overseas offices to select a national charity operating in their country in a similar field.) The charity committee did very valuable work, not only in supporting worthwhile causes, but also in fostering a strong team spirit amongst staff.

A more local charity which we supported at Teddington was the Thames Community Foundation. Shortly after the company was formed I had been introduced to its chief executive, Sandy Gilmour, by our bank, HSBC, and I had offered support to this locally-based initiative by providing office space for the charity in one of the Victorian houses adjacent to LGC's main laboratory building. I became good friends with Sandy who, I was to discover, had an amazing number of contacts in industry, the media, and the city. He kindly introduced me and LGC to some of them and helped spread the word about our company.

Our investment agreement with 3i required us to pay a proportion of our profits as a dividend on 'A' ordinary shares owned by them and the

RSC. However, although no dividend payments were made in the first year, as a consequence of the steady growth in the company the board felt it right to pay a small dividend to staff shareholders (ordinary shares and 'B' ordinary shares). We were also required to arrange for our auditors to conduct an annual valuation of our shares to allow staff who left us to sell their shares through the Employment Benefit Trust I had established, and new staff to buy them. Each year the share value increased. In time it registered with staff that the shares that they had purchased when the company was formed or had been awarded under our share option scheme were becoming a valuable asset. The success of the company and its growth was reflected in a substantial increase in the value of their shares.

One aspect of our investment agreements with 3i and RSC was that if the Company were to redeem its preference shares ahead of the agreed schedule, the institutional shareholders would cancel some of their 'A' ordinary shares. So in December 1999, during our fourth year of successful trading during which we had redeemed all our preference shares, 16,800 'A' ordinary shares were cancelled. Two months later many staff took up their option to purchase shares. This was a very significant milestone. A high proportion of staff had now become shareholders, thereby fulfilling my original vision of a company partly owned by its staff.

There had been major changes in our staffing and a new management structure had been introduced but, with the exception of Adrian Wilson's retirement and his replacement by Clive Hall, there had been no changes to our small board on which there was a majority of non-executive directors. I felt it was desirable to have some rotation and, after discussion with our 'institutional' shareholders and individual board members, I tentatively raised the question at the board. The contracts I had agreed with the chairman and other two non-executives were for a period of three years and we were now at this point. Board changes are not always easy, but I was grateful that Jack Betteridge, RSC's nominee, agreed willingly to stand down at the AGM in September 1999; he was replaced by Dr John Beacham, who had by now retired from ICI.

When the company was formed it had been agreed that 3i would act for the institutional investors in monitoring financial progress, while RSC, through its Advisory Committee, would confine its interest to the company's science. Jack Betteridge had helped create the Advisory Committee, which was chaired by Brian Pierce, a council member of RSC's analytical division, and included members with experience of a wide range of analytical science. The Committee met each quarter and received regular presentations from the company. Each year it organised an audit and monitored LGC's scientific progress against a series of benchmarks. It was gratifying that the annual audits reported good progress on all fronts and highly praised the company's scientific achievements. Together with the regular audits of our quality systems by accreditation and certification bodies and others, these annual audits conducted by the RSC strongly reinforced our status as a national centre of excellence.

The new strategic plan and the initiatives which flowed from it had a dramatic effect on the organisation. Our early acquisitions had helped rapidly to build the Group (the term by which we now referred collectively to the companies which we had set up or acquired) and our success in expanding our forensic work for the police and winning new contracts in all parts of our business further boosted the organisation. There was no longer any doubt that the organisation could flourish as a private company; our early success was now breeding further success. During our fifth year as a company, we completed the first year of a major contract for the Child Support Agency providing paternity testing services, and the team that had joined us from ICI won a significant outsourcing contract for Infineum, a company specialising in the development and marketing of oil additives. What became a particularly significant contract was a 10-year agreement with the Medicines Control Agency (now called the Medicines and Healthcare products Regulatory Agency (MHRA)) to establish dedicated laboratory facilities for them at Teddington. This opportunity had been identified by Ray Ah-Sun and had taken a long time to come to fruition. Its importance was that it was a genuine public/private partnership, with LGC providing staff and facilities and MHRA funding equipment and steering the work according to the changing priorities of the Agency. The arrangement worked well, providing improved services to MHRA at a lower cost. The unusual length of the contract provided LGC with long-term security of income and our relationship with MHRA subsequently developed with the provision of a second laboratory at Teddington for the British Pharmacopeia.

Another major public-sector contract win was the provision of genotyping services to MAFF under the National Scrapie Plan. The background to this was the BSE crisis and MAFF's desire to eradicate scrapie, a disease in sheep which had been known about for years and had similarities to BSE. It had been discovered that sheep with a particular genetic make-up were resistant to scrapie. By selecting such sheep for breeding (and not using sheep with genetic types which indicated a predisposition to develop scrapie) it was planned to eradicate the disease from the UK. (Interestingly, New Zealand sheep did not appear to develop scrapie.) In being briefed on the subject, I learned that there is a class system in sheep; 'upper class' sheep belong to registered pedigree flocks and are only allowed to breed amongst themselves whereas the lowest class of sheep are free to roam and breed with any sheep they encounter! The aim of the National Scrapie Plan was to start by genotyping top-class sheep and then work down.

In preparing for this major tender we investigated several different technologies from 'conventional' gene sequencing, as used in our forensic DNA laboratory, to an advanced technology developed by a Californian company called Sequenon which used mass spectrometry. This technology had been developed for the human genome project; LGC's entrepreneurial move was to consider applying it to mass genetic screening. It was ideally suited to large numbers of samples (over 1m per year) but less economic than current technology for lower numbers. There were risks involved, but we worked hard with Sequenon to demonstrate the huge advantages of a novel approach. We submitted a sophisticated bid, setting out in full the science and the logistics involved in this new programme and showing how we would apply 'conventional' gene sequencing, or alternatively the novel mass spectrometry method. This allowed MAFF to choose which approach they wanted to adopt.

We now had a track record of handling large numbers of samples, for police forensic work and for our veterinary residues contract, and we had expended effort investigating systems for monitoring and controlling processes at every stage. We now had impressive bar coding and IT systems to demonstrate to the team that came to inspect our operations. It was clear that their scientific advisers were impressed by the novel method we proposed and they took time to examine every detail of our proposal. When the contract was awarded, MAFF decided to divide the work between ourselves and Cellmark, the company I had wanted to acquire which was now owned by the US company, Orchid. MAFF clearly wanted to reduce their risk by opting for two technologies, asking Cellmark to use 'conventional' gene sequencing and LGC to use the latest, but less proven, technology. Winning half the work in a large programme was a major achievement and we rapidly geared up to receive our first samples.

The contract required substantial investment in robotic systems to extract DNA from rather sticky sheep's blood and ultimately to place minute spots of a few nanolitres (a thousand millionth of a litre) of amplified DNA on a silicon chip to be bombarded by a laser for a split second before analysis of the scattered fragments in a sophisticated mass spectrometer. The programme started well, but after a few weeks our quality system picked up an anomalous result, unfortunately not before it had been reported to the sheep farmer who had submitted samples for testing. A quick investigation identified several such anomalies and I was informed immediately. I did not hesitate in phoning MAFF within minutes of hearing that it was possible that we could have misinformed several farmers of the genetic make-up of some of their sheep, and MAFF rightly directed all samples to the other contractor until we had investigated the problem fully.

Unusually, the scrapie misreporting incident was not a result of human error (usually the cause of very rare errors) but arose from a technical glitch which we luckily managed to spot at a very early stage. The investigation took some time because we had identified a problem with using mass spectrometry which had not previously been encountered. Fortunately, our genetic scientists were able to consult some of Europe's most experienced mass spectroscopists who worked in another team at LGC. Dr Gavin O'Connor and his colleagues provided an explanation of interference between different genetic fragments with identical mass numbers, and were able to help our geneticists overcome the problem. However, this was, unfortunately, not before Parliamentary Questions had been asked on behalf of some irate farmers. It was several weeks before we were able to reassure MAFF and their technical experts that we had sorted out a problem which had never been observed previously, and we were able to resume the programme. Although we suffered considerably from a financial point of view, at the end of this incident our reputation with our customer was enhanced, not least by the fact that we had reported the problem immediately it had been discovered, that we had been completely open throughout our investigation, and we had been able to rectify a technical problem which had hitherto not been encountered. The contract continued smoothly and efficiently thereafter. The incident was an example of how the prompt and careful handling of an error or complaint does not just mitigate the damage caused but can, perverse as it may seem, actually enhance the reputation of a company. We used this as an example of how customer care was such an important ingredient in LGC's success.

An error in a report is the nightmare of every laboratory director. Although LGC had incredibly thorough quality systems based on internationally agreed certification and accreditation systems, and rarely a day went by when we were not receiving auditors for inspection of one part or another of our organisation, errors still occurred, albeit very, very rarely. From the moment I arrived at LGC I had taken a close interest in quality and safety, not least because our reputation rested on our claim to be 'setting standards in analytical science'. Our quality and safety manager reported directly to me and I had raised the status of the position when I appointed to the post John Day, a highly experienced laboratory manager with broad scientific experience. I frequently discussed with John what improvements we should make and how we could be sure we remained in the top league. Of the very small number of quality or safety incidents, most were directly or indirectly a consequence of human error. I believed that you could not rely on certification and accreditation systems alone to minimise the possibility of such error. Indeed, I frequently spoke on the subject at international gatherings, criticising the quality bandwagon that had been created by accreditation bodies who, without consideration of cost, constantly introduced new rules and new boxes that had to be ticked. Although I fully supported basic quality systems and external inspections, and I recognised that laboratory procedures and protocols were important, in my view behavioural factors were at the heart of ensuring quality and safety. I argued that an excess of written instructions led to de-skilling of staff by introducing a culture that ranked box-ticking ahead of the application of good sense. Over the years we tried various benchmarking and business excellence systems and, in relation to safety, we aimed for, and were awarded, prestigious awards by the Royal Society for the Prevention of Accidents (RoSPA). We were proud of these achievements, but I never rested on these laurels and continued in my firm belief that staff selection, training and development were vital in these and all aspects of our business. The culture I strove to create was one of professional standards, openness, honesty, and continuous improvement.

Our reputation for quality and technical expertise was illustrated by an incident which had hugely important consequences. In June 2001 I received a phone call from Dr David Shannon, the Chief Scientist at the Department of Environment, Food and Rural Affairs (Defra), asking me whether LGC had DNA analysis techniques which could distinguish between brain tissue from sheep and tissue from cattle, and whether LGC could detect contamination of ovine brain tissue with a very small quantity of bovine brain tissue. He explained that a major research investigation into whether BSE had been transferred to sheep had involved feeding a 'pooled' sample of sheep brain tissue to mice. If the mice developed BSE this would show that the disease had crossed species from infected cows to sheep. David Shannon told me in strict confidence that the preliminary results of this experiment led to the devastating conclusion that sheep had become infected with BSE. The probable consequence of this would be the mass cull of Britain's flock of 35 million sheep and lambs, which would be catastrophic for British farming and would cause widespread fear among consumers.

Defra wanted to scrutinise every aspect of the study and, since the pooled sample had been stored for 10 years, wanted to check whether there was any possibility that it could have been contaminated with a very small amount of brain material from cows. I was surprised that there was any doubt about the authenticity of the sample, but fully understood why a check, even right at the end of the five-year research project, was so vitally important.

I agreed that LGC would take on the work and a small team led by Helen Parkes, who had pioneered LGC's development of analytical molecular biology, liaised with the Institute of Animal Health which had undertaken the research study. She obtained reference samples of certain origin so that we could develop robust analytical procedures. Although Defra was impatient for the answer, we knew that whatever results we found, LGC's reputation would be on the line. After painstaking validation studies and measurements of the actual sample, Helen Parkes came to see me one Friday evening with the astonishing news that our results indicated that the sample in question had not just been contaminated with brain from cows; it appeared to be <u>pure</u> bovine material. That weekend, the experiments were repeated, but the following Tuesday, we were absolutely certain that the totally unexpected and extraordinary result was correct. It appeared that the material which had been fed to mice over the duration of the study was not the pooled brains of sheep; unbelievably, it was the pooled brains of cows. Our result had exposed a huge blunder by the Institute of Animal Health, but thanks to our work, millions of sheep and lambs now appeared to be safe from slaughter.

Helen went to Defra to present her findings to a high-level scientific committee and was subjected to aggressive questioning about our work. She stood her ground, however, and that night Defra's Secretary of State, Margaret Beckett, issued a statement. The press and media were not slow to cotton on to the magnitude of the error which led to five years of research into the possibility of BSE in sheep being scrapped. There were headlines in every newspaper.

Despite the potential for publicity which would hugely have enhanced our reputation by highlighting LGC's key role in averting a major food crisis, preventing a disaster for farming, and saving countless sheep from slaughter, I decided that we should adopt a low profile in dealing with the press. It seemed wrong that we should seek to take advantage of an error made by another scientific organisation; we should keep out of the fray and retain our position of independence and impartiality and not join in the witch hunt. We placed our technical report on our website and issued a very short statement. Sadly, the Institute of Animal Health initially disputed our findings; this led to my first and only letter to the scientific journal Nature on the subject of DNA analysis.

Although we had chosen to shun the spotlight, our highly professional work, based on robust and validated analytical science, was recognised throughout government and our reputation for 'setting standards' was, understandably, greatly strengthened. Our work was often referred to by Sir David King, the Government's Chief Scientific Adviser, and Lord (David) Sainsbury whom I had separately invited to visit LGC around the time of this incident.

It is now perhaps a little difficult to recall the huge political sensitivity over food safety which extended throughout the 1990s. The disastrous handling of the BSE crisis and the public's understandable concern over the provenance and processing of food had led to the creation by the new Labour Government of the Food Standards Agency (FSA). The professionalism and openness of the FSA removed food safety from the front line of politics. FSA developed a reputation for independence and for providing advice based on sound scientific evidence. It was rightly cautious in its approach, and it did not pretend that it was possible to claim zero risk, as John Gummer, then Minister of Agriculture, had famously and injudiciously tried to do when he fed a hamburger to his young daughter in 1990, at the height of the BSE scare. The public wanted assurance of absolute safety, but the FSA stuck to its guns in explaining that nothing was without risk; consumers should be aware of the balance of risk so that they could make their own informed decisions. The agency cautiously entered the difficult area of nutritional advice and managed to steer a sensible line between improving public awareness and avoiding accusations of being part of the nanny state.

Our growing reputation undoubtedly contributed to other contract wins for both private and public sector organisations. After a long period of discussions, the Department of Health (DoH) decided to outsource to LGC the management of their R&D programme on New and Emerging Applications of Technology. This was the beginning of what was to become a long-term relationship, with parallels to our successful partnership with the Medicines and Healthcare products Regulation Agency, under which LGC took on the management of several other DoH programmes. However, another major contract for which we bid would require extensive investment in new laboratories and was to be a huge step in LGC's development.

Early in 2001 Defra asked for 'expressions of interest' in supplying analytical services to test all slaughtered cattle over 30 months old to establish whether they had traces of BSE in their brain stems. The programme was prompted by work postulating a connection between new variant Creutzfeldt-Jakob disease (CJD) in humans and consumption of beef infected with BSE. The first line of defence in the protection of public health was the removal from all carcasses of neural tissue (where the BSE agent was most likely to be found). Testing samples from the brain stems of carcasses of younger cattle was not proposed since BSE had not been found in animals less than 30 months old. The testing that Defra was introducing for older cattle (which were not at this stage allowed to enter the food chain) had been recommended by the Food Standards Agency and was part of a European Union-wide programme.

Our decision to bid for this work was not taken lightly. The logistics involved in receiving samples from approved slaughter-houses over the UK throughout the day, analysing the samples during the evening and overnight, and ensuring results were with the slaughter-houses by the following morning, were not straightforward. We evaluated the various testing methods which had been approved by the European Commission and negotiated terms with suppliers for test kits and other consumables which we had thoroughly evaluated. The bulky tender document that we submitted covered in detail every aspect of the delivery of this high-profile national programme. However, one of the most difficult aspects was the pricing decision. The initial contract was to be for just one year. In order to undertake the work we would have to convert and equip a laboratory at Teddington operating to very high standards of hygiene, both to protect our staff and to avoid any possibility of BSE agents escaping. The ventilation of the laboratories, protective clothing and the treatment of wastes were all considered in great detail.

Making sure that samples would be taken correctly in the abattoirs, packed securely in tamper-proof containers and then dispatched in packages that were strong enough to resist rough handling in transit was a major challenge, but there was great satisfaction for all involved in finding foolproof solutions for a programme which we knew would be inspected in every minute detail. Fortunately, the LIMS systems which we had developed for our growing DNA testing and scrapie genotyping businesses could be adapted to the need to track each sample at each stage in the process. Our IT experts evaluated every step in the process, from the provision of bar-coded sample containers to slaughterhouses, through gathering key information and delivery of samples to LGC, to monitoring every stage of the analytical process and transmitting results with a traffic light system (red for infected cattle, green for cattle that could be released for food, and amber for a suspect result or incomplete sample) to the abattoirs. The start-up costs were considerable and we decided we had to write them off over the one year of the contract, even though there was a reasonable chance the contract would be extended.

As with the scrapie contract, I led the small team which presented our proposal to officials from Defra and their advisers. I felt incredibly proud of my colleagues' presentations and the way they answered questions, which showed breadth of scientific understanding, experience of logistics, and a strong focus on customer requirements. The period of elation after we were informed of the favourable outcome of the tender process was brief; after signing the contract we had just six weeks to get everything in place to begin work. During this period our new BSE testing laboratory was completely fitted out and equipped and staff identified and trained. The programme began on time and our performance confirmed our technical proficiency and organisational ability. Aware that if anything had gone wrong the press would have shown no mercy, Defra were delighted that BSE testing in the UK had been introduced without a hitch and we subsequently received visits from Sir John Krebs, Chairman of the Food Standards Agency, and received very positive audit reports from everyone who came to inspect the programme, including the European Commission.

Planning and managing the BSE testing programme was interesting and challenging at every level. The science was relatively new and our choice of test (initially a kit manufactured by an Irish company, Enfer) was crucial. Staff needed to be trained and the key managers worked night shifts at Enfer's laboratories in Ireland so that they became familiar with every aspect of the process. The robotics and laboratory processes were complex, but the logistics involved in the collection of samples from all over the country and delivery of results – we consulted widely on this and for a period retained a logistics expert – were very challenging. The senior scientists involved, Ian Lumley and Peter Farnell, (both of whom, incidentally, had undergone the night shift training in Ireland so that they had a full understanding of the testing procedures) approached all aspects of programme management in an immensely professional way, getting as much satisfaction from devising hub-and-spoke logistics models which transported samples from remote locations all over the country to our laboratory at Teddington within a few hours, as from planning the laboratory processes. Time was a crucial factor, since we had to supply results to allow abattoirs to release carcasses shortly after dawn the day after the sample had been taken, and there were constant efforts to shave minutes off each stage of the whole operation. Ian and Peter, both thoughtful and calm individuals who inspired trust, played key roles with Defra in communicating with stakeholders, including farmers, abattoir owners, the Food Standards Agency, and the European Commission. Later, the manager in charge of the BSE programme showed immense patience in dealing with problems (not usually relating to LGC) which could arise at any time during the day or night, and the huge professionalism LGC showed in managing this complex programme led to our contract being renewed. The statistics that we produced and analysed for Defra were important in the future framing of policy in this area.

Alongside the development of new services, we were constantly looking for new science and technology which could form the basis of our future growth. Dr John Marriott, who joined us in 2000 from Courtaulds, and Dr Paul Debenham, who had joined us as head of University Diagnostics, together with other scientists including Dr Derek Craston, head of our small strategic research team, Tim Catterick, head of our trace analysis team, and Helen Parkes, head of our analytical molecular biology research team all had suggestions for new scientific areas we should investigate, and we held occasional science away days to generate new ideas. In the field of high accuracy measurement, John Marriott reviewed a range of up-and-coming mass spectroscopic techniques and we invested heavily in this area, becoming probably one of the leading laboratories in the world in the application of mass spectroscopy.

Our purchase of an advanced inductively coupled plasma mass spectrometer (ICP-MS) for trace element analysis, which had been approved at one of the first meetings of the board of the new company, had sent a strong signal of our commitment to scientific studies in this field. LGC's subsequent performance in inter-laboratory comparisons between international institutes, under the auspices of the BIPM, was very strong. The team we built up, with scientists from several different countries, to work using isotope dilution mass spectrometry (IDMS) for very precise measurements at very low levels, established a world-class position. As a consequence of our expertise in this area, we were invited to take part in clinical studies on selenium in the diet and in supplements. Selenium is an important trace mineral which is found in certain plants, seafood and meat. A decline in the use of selenium-rich wheat flour from North

America has contributed to a substantial fall in the amount of selenium in the European diet. Studies show that too little selenium in the diet increases the risk of developing cancer; however, too much causes toxic effects such as loss of hair and damage to the heart. Selenium is a difficult element to analyse at low levels and its chemical form determines whether and how it is metabolised. LGC's work on selenium in yeast and a range of other foods has contributed to a better understanding of the biological effects of selenium and the mechanism of its anti-cancer activity. Our work has also led to the production of a reference material which can be used as a standard by other laboratories undertaking work in this area. In showing visitors round our Teddington laboratories, this was an area with highly advanced instrumentation and excellent scientific staff of which I was always very proud.

In addition to mass spectrometry, we were constantly on the lookout for promising opportunities in other scientific areas, especially biochemical analysis. Among the developments we pursued was a technique for rapid genetic analysis which we called HyBeacons. Although LGC is primarily a service organisation, HyBeacons was among a small number of innovations we were able to patent. HyBeacons took many years to develop; initially its application appeared to be in rapid medical diagnostics (such as for chlamydia) but more recently it has been shown to have considerable potential in forensic DNA profiling.

During periods of rapid growth it is more difficult to keep tight control over costs than during periods of retrenchment. Starting up new areas of work often requires additional resources, and our experience with the first year of the VMD contract illustrated how costs could escalate. However, our corporate plan not only set targets for sales growth but also envisaged a steady increase in profitability. Staff salaries were the largest single component of our costs and we relentlessly sought ways of increasing operational efficiency. Where possible we used the activity value analysis technique, which we had applied in the pre-privatisation operational review, to examine all 'discretionary' activities and identify where savings might be made. As a consequence of continuous investment in IT systems, in particular in our Laboratory Information Management System (LIMS), we were able to make substantial savings in the administrative costs of laboratory operations, and wherever possible we invested in automation. Many of our staff became skilled at examining how work flowed through our laboratories, and they identified often quite simple changes which could substantially increase efficiency. (Later a small team was set up with the specific task of examining and modelling laboratory processes and working with the laboratory staff involved to come up with improved ways of working.) Some of our staff visited other organisations in different fields to glean ideas for productivity improvements, and we had a suggestions scheme with small rewards for staff who came forward with improvement proposals. The staff most knowledgeable about an activity or process are those actually doing the work, and in my view it is essential that they should be fully involved in efforts to improve productivity and reduce costs. With some outside help in analysing processes, small groups of staff can often come up with sensible and imaginative improvements. Of course, since many staff were shareholders, there was an added incentive for everyone to be economical in the use of resources.

The first years of the millennium saw a transformation in LGC. My vision of a vibrant science-based service company, partly owned by its staff, and expanding in the UK and throughout Europe, had become a reality. My efforts, and those of my colleagues at all levels in the company, had shown that it was possible to create a successful business with a strong reputation for science and a highly professional approach to the practical problems of collecting samples and delivering results. We had applied new scientific methodology in entrepreneurial ways and this had contributed to our winning major contracts such as for testing for veterinary medicines and genotyping sheep. We had developed business outside the UK and our name and brand were gaining a reputation for quality and customer service. Although our 'framework agreement' with DTI ended after five years, our success in winning work from many different private and public sector bodies more than compensated for the loss of the safety net this agreement had provided. By the end of 2001/2 our sales were over £40M, nearly three times more than when the Company was formed. However, this was no bubble; we had invested in people and equipment for the long term and the prospects were excellent. We were on course to achieving the corporate plan goals we had set ourselves and to reaching our target of becoming a £100 million turnover company.

Chapter 6: *Coming of age*

Changes at the top – Exit of The Royal Society of Chemistry and a new share structure– Pay and rewards – Building organisational infrastructure – A new Government Chemist – Values – The science of BSE testing– Competing with a dominant government-owned supplier – Further expansion in Europe

On Monday 2nd April 2001, five years and a day after the new company I had formed began trading, all staff were greeted on their arrival at work by me or another director who handed them a gerbera flower and a card thanking them for their contribution to LGC's success. (The vast majority of staff greatly appreciated this, although there were inevitably a few cynics who thought the gesture a waste of money.) LGC had achieved far more than anyone, including me, could have anticipated. We had cast off the negative aspects of our public sector legacy, established our core values, and had achieved recognition as a leading science service company.

With the retirement of Adrian Wilson as finance director and the change in the Royal Society of Chemistry's board representation, there was some new blood on our board, but there had been no further rotation of non-executive board members. As we approached the five-year milestone, I had discussions with our chairman, Sir Brian Richards, and he volunteered to stand down when we had found a suitable replacement. Brian had been a supportive chairman who had been particularly interested in the growth of our DNA business. However, our relationship had been quite distant. In many ways it had had suited me that he simply attended board meetings and occasional events and left me free to manage and shape the company in the way I saw fit. However, there were some big issues on the horizon that I needed to address and (while still not wanting too much interference in running my own show) I was keen that the new chairman should bring a fresh, external perspective to them.

I turned to 3i for help in finding a new chairman. At the time they had an excellent unit for identifying non-executive directors which was led by Patrick Dunne, an expert on boardroom issues. They sent me some cvs and I invited three people to visit LGC at Teddington. By far the best, in my view, was Ian Kent. He had broad experience of the pharmaceutical, biotechnology, food science and agrochemicals sectors and, as former chairman of the Intervention Board, also had experience of working with government. He had a 'portfolio' of non-executive directorships of private companies and had been involved in fundraising and corporate transactions. By chance, Ian had taken over from Brian Richards as chairman of the Roslyn Institute and Brian thought he would be an excellent successor. Ian joined the board in May 2001, overlapping with Brian before taking over as chairman in July.

Ian made an almost immediate impact with respect to our shareholders. My relationship with 3i had not been bad, but I had been unimpressed by the frequency with which 3i had changed the managers assigned to LGC. I did not always find their advice helpful, nor did I appreciate their hints that LGC should be increasing in value as fast as the technology companies in which 3i had recently invested. 3i organised a series of seminars and events where I met directors of other investee companies. By comparison with many of the technology companies at the time that were rapidly increasing in value (if not in profitability), LGC was admittedly rather unexciting from an investor point of view. At a dinner hosted by Baroness Hogg in the House of Lords there was much discussion of the 'new economy' based on the internet. Although I was able to make LGC (especially its DNA profiling forensic work) sound interesting, I was unable to promise the exponential growth over a very short period of time that leaders of new internet companies around the dinner table were cheerily predicting for themselves. There seemed to be little challenge to the thesis that the immediate future was entirely with the internet and that all conventional businesses were about to expire. I found it difficult not to be cynical when some of the companies which were not profitable were regarded as superior to mine which was achieving steady and increasing returns. (I admit to a touch of schadenfreude when the technology bubble burst shortly afterwards.) Ian knew 3i well and recognised that LGC would benefit from a change of contact there. He quickly arranged that we should be transferred to the technology and health care team that operated from 3i's Cambridge office. It was a breath of fresh air and 3i's approach to LGC improved overnight.

LGC: The making of a company

LGC's relationship with the Royal Society of Chemistry was less straightforward. Their Secretary General, Dr Tom Inch, had enthusiastically supported my management buy-out and he understood what I was trying to achieve at LGC and was impressed by the company's rapid development. However, many people in the Society were less convinced, and obtaining permissions required by our shareholder agreements, for example for an acquisition, was always a laborious process since the RSC had to adhere to restrictions arising from its charitable status. Moreover, having been badly bruised by its membership when the Society initially invested in LGC, their officials were worried about any business move that could re-inflame the objectors. When he retired in 2000 Tom was replaced by Dr David Giachardi, whom I had known a little when he was a director of Courtaulds. Not having been involved in the company's genesis, David understandably had no particular commitment to LGC and he showed little interest in the company's development. After a rather frustrating period when we discussed how LGC might substitute for the payment of dividends the provision of services of a similar value, a suggestion which was initially welcomed but subsequently turned down, the board agreed that John Beacham, the RSC's representative on our board, might broach the subject of RSC exiting by selling its shares in LGC. Slightly to our surprise, the Society felt the time was right for them to sever financial links with LGC and their treasurer, Barry Price, asked PricewaterhouseCoopers (PwC) to advise them on the value of their shares. A deal was finally agreed which effectively involved the buy-back of RSC's shares at a price (yielding a return of over £2 million) which took account of the fact that selling a minority stake reduced the value of these shares. The deal with the RSC allowed a share restructuring to be agreed at an Extraordinary General Meeting in August 2002, attended by many staff shareholders. The resolution involved cancellation of the repaid preference shares and some of RSC's ordinary shares, and the creation of a special dividend share for 3i which limited their dividend rights to the position before RSC sold their shares. 3i and, with a loan from the Company, the Employee Benefit Trust purchased more shares and we split old shares into 10 new shares, largely to make our balance sheet look more sensible. The end result was that staff, together with the Employee Benefit Trust, now owned a substantial majority of the shares in the company. This model of staff ownership was what I had envisioned at the outset.

Initially, the other agreements between RSC, DTI and LGC, under which the Society supported an Advisory Committee to monitor the work of the Government Chemist and the scientific quality of the organisation, continued unchanged; they were later to be amended to end all links with RSC. In selling their shares, the RSC had made a return of many times its initial investment, which could be used for the benefit of chemistry. I had hoped that the Society would create something like an LGC bursary in recognition of this, but the substantial financial benefit that LGC had brought to the Society was, sadly, never acknowledged except as a minor footnote in their annual accounts.

From the outset, a particular issue I had to address was senior management pay. Formally, my own pay was determined by the remuneration committee of the board and I advised the committee on the pay of other senior managers. When I formed the company, I was adamant that we should not follow the example of many newly privatised organisations by introducing massive reward packages for senior managers. During the early years of the company I recommended only modest pay rises in base pay and, much to the bemusement of my non-executive board colleagues, I declined a pay rise that they had recommended for me. We introduced a bonus scheme for senior managers which provided for bonuses of up to 20% of base salary, half relating to corporate performance and half relating to the achievement of personal objectives. Each year I prepared a detailed paper for the remuneration committee with my pay and bonus recommendations and argued that rewards had to take into account the potentially large long-term benefits of owning shares.

By comparison with other similar-sized companies (we subscribed to some pay surveys) our senior pay was modest. I was more concerned to improve the starting salaries of recently qualified scientists and felt that it would be wrong for senior pay hugely to outstrip that of other staff who were working hard to make a success of the new company. In recruiting new staff I always emphasised the unique culture of an employee-owned organisation, rather than tempting people to join us with the prospect of large salaries. However, with the need to recruit experienced managers, there was constant pressure to increase senior pay and introduce other benefits such as company cars (another move that I resisted for as long as I could). Over time the pressure built up to do something about the reward of senior managers. Dennis Stocks had always felt that the management had not got a sufficiently large slice of the cake when the company was formed and that RSC and 3i had been given an incredibly good deal under the initial investment agreements. He had raised with 3i the possibility of a share management incentive plan which would be linked to the share value when the institutional shareholders sold their shares. RSC's decision to exit and sell their shares provided the opportunity to replace this scheme by a senior management share option plan involving an option price above the current value of shares.

We also introduced wider bonus schemes. At the end of successful years all employees were given a fixed bonus determined by the board, and we introduced various bonus schemes for individual managers and discretionary bonuses for people who had excelled on a specific project. Although I was keen to reward exceptional work, I was well aware of the de-motivating (as well as motivating) consequences of bonus schemes. Most people at LGC worked in teams, and team rewards, rather than individual rewards, were less divisive. Many, including me, were already working flat out, so that large financial incentives were not going to make much difference, except possibly to distort behaviour towards achieving personal targets set at the beginning of the year which, by the end of the year, might not necessarily turn out to be the most important things to achieve. I was keen to improve general levels of pay; scientific staff are not highly paid compared with staff in other professions such as accountancy and law. On the other hand, I have always felt it right to reward real achievement and, for this purpose, bonuses are often preferable to large increases in base salary. Achieving the right balance is an essential part of establishing the culture of an organisation.

Sorting out the relationship with our shareholders and our balance sheet enabled Ian Kent and me to consider the company structure and management talent. At the time of Ian's arrival in 2001 the board consisted of three non-executive directors and two executive directors, myself and Clive Hall, the relatively new finance director. Although individual managers attended the board for particular agenda items, Dennis Stocks had always felt that a stronger executive presence would be beneficial in removing some of the pressure from me. The most obvious candidate was Ray Ah-Sun who, as head of business development, had made a hugely creative contribution to LGC's development. We worked incredibly well together and I always listened to his advice. However, I felt his time was much better spent forging relationships outside the organisation than in dealing with corporate issues, and this was the role he enjoyed. The other possible board appointment was John Mason, who had moved from Teddington to take charge of our operations in the Northwest and was closely involved with organisational matters. He had a good understanding of the company and was in tune with the ethical, yet entrepreneurial, culture I was trying to create. So, as part of a reorganisation which involved the appointment of divisional directors, John Mason, at that time not only Managing Director of LGC's northwest operations but also Director of Chemicals, Water and Environment Division, joined the board in April 2002 as an executive director.

Later in 2002, after a long search process, Dr Nigel Law was appointed Director, Group Operations. A scientist by background, Nigel had held various operations, planning and marketing roles with Exxon Mobil, in addition to a period with Mercer management consultancy, before joining Hoyer, the transport and logistics company. Nigel's arrival coincided with the appointment of a further non-executive director, in addition to Ian Kent, Dennis Stocks and John Beacham. Marion Sears had begun her career in pharmaceutical marketing at Glaxo before moving to the City, where she had worked in stockbroking and then healthcare investment banking at JP Morgan until the previous year. The strengthening of our board was accompanied by some key appointments throughout the organisation.

One move which I had been considering for some time was the appointment of a new Government Chemist. I had held the post of Government Chemist since I joined the Laboratory of the Government Chemist, then part of DTI, in 1991. As part of privatisation arrangements, I was reappointed Government Chemist by DTI's Secretary of State in 1996 for a further five years. My contract had been further extended in 2001 but I had indicated then that I wished to separate the role of Government Chemist from that of chief executive of LGC and that DTI should appoint a successor. After much discussion with DTI officials and representatives of the Royal Society of Chemistry (who had responsibility for overseeing the role) it was recommended that Dr John Marriott should be appointed, although it was recognised that future appointments would have to be subject to the new public appointments procedures which were being introduced in response to the (Nolan) Committee on Standards in Public Life. When he joined LGC in 2000 John brought with him wide experience of science and management from his previous career at Courtaulds and during his time with us he had developed a better grasp of the issues facing analytical science than probably anyone else in the UK. So, after eleven years as Government Chemist (the same period in office as the first Government Chemist, Sir James Dobbie, who held the post between 1909 and 1920) I handed the reins over to John Marriott, enabling me to concentrate entirely on running LGC.

My time leading LGC was almost entirely positive – developing plans for growth, winning new work and appointing new staff. But a rapidly growing business is not without its stresses; it involves constant reappraisal and constant change. The changes in our shareholding and board structure were necessary because of LGC's strong growth, but there was little time to draw breath. During 2002/3 LGC's sales grew by a further 26% and broke through the £50 million barrier, and operating profit increased by over 80%.

Adapting to the change from being a relatively small unit based at Teddington to a Group of companies in the UK and now in Europe required changes to our infrastructure. Our Laboratory Information Management System (LIMS) was serving us well with our new work, but we needed better management information. After a lot of analysis, we embarked on changing our financial information system, never an easy task. Needless to say, as seems inevitable with IT systems, it took longer to install, and was more expensive, than we had planned. Nevertheless, it was an important move, since timely and accurate management information is essential to running and controlling a business.

We also made changes to our building at Teddington. We had already used space vacated during our operational review in the run-up to privatisation for our new DNA, veterinary residue analysis, MHRA and BSE laboratories. We had created open-plan offices to replace numerous individual offices, to make space for the new staff we were recruiting in finance and programme management teams. However, I had long argued that we needed a small restaurant in which our predominantly young staff could meet for refreshment. I felt that such a facility would encourage exchanges, professional as well as social, between staff from different parts of the company and could provide an informal setting for meetings over coffee or lunch. Earlier, the board had rejected a proposal I had made to open a restaurant (almost the only occasion when they had gone against me) on the grounds of cost, but I remained convinced that such a facility would facilitate communication throughout the company and would be of positive benefit to staff and visitors. The second time I proposed such a scheme, my colleagues on the board approved the expenditure, albeit still rather reluctantly. The small restaurant was planned in great detail by Andrew French (our building manager), his assistant Maggie Burns, Lorna Hopkinson-Hall (my PA) and me; we visited a number of other similar facilities and chose the furniture together. A competition amongst staff to name the restaurant was won by Imelda Topping, who suggested 'Helix' to recognise the 50th anniversary that year of the discovery of DNA.

Helix was an instant success; the restaurant provided good cold food and a hot menu at lunchtime and provided an excellent informal meeting place for all staff. It was frequently used for meetings and, like others, I often took my guests to lunch there. The non-executive directors, who had questioned whether the expense could be justified, readily recognised the value of having an attractive communal place for everyone to meet during the day. Many years later a member of staff featured in 'The hot seat', a regular item in the staff newsletter, LGC News, gave as his answer to the question 'What's one of the best things about LGC?': 'I have always felt that LGC has a 'family feel' about it. I can walk into Helix and have several conversations with a host of different colleagues or acquaintances.' That is exactly what Helix was created for.

There are often debates about the merits of centralising services, for example152 for marketing and human resources, as against devolving responsibility to operational divisions. As LGC grew, it was natural that some support services should be provided by operational divisions so that there was a closer connection with the 'front line'. However, I felt the company was insufficiently mature to allow the divisions complete freedom to promote their services and recruit staff. I wanted to ensure a single brand across the whole Group. I hoped that through training, such as the Ashridge course, we could be more confident about the quality of decisions made at all levels, but at this stage I certainly remained very 'hands-on' and was personally involved in all major business moves and all managerial recruitment. I worked on almost all major tenders and took part in pricing decisions, since they presented not only opportunities, but potential risks, to the company. I also involved myself in some quite detailed issues such as the design of the staff restaurant which I thought would be an important statement of LGC's culture. I spent time with individual staff throughout the Group, encouraging and guiding them so that they had direct feedback from the top of the organisation.

Although I recognised that organisational structures were important (it is obviously important that people should know who is boss), I was cautious about changing the organisational framework without good reason. I wanted to encourage a culture which involved working across organisational boundaries and I didn't want staff to be obsessed by positions or grades; rather, I wanted a common set of values to be understood and accepted. New chief executives (and especially politicians in charge of the National Health Service) often feel obliged radically to change the organisation, in the belief (or rather, hope) that this will improve efficiency, save costs, or whatever. However, in my experience, it is the culture, values and behaviour of the people who make up the organisation that have the greatest influence on performance. Changing the organisational wiring diagram is quick and easy; changing the culture and values is a more subtle and longer-term process.

With this in mind a group of staff who had been on the Ashridge course, led by Jo Bloomfield, our Head of Marketing, and Jane Firth, now in charge of the Pentagon Programme, set about trying to articulate a list of 'values' which were core to the organisation; they had observed how other successful companies had worked hard to define their values and embed them throughout their organisation. I knew how difficult it was to define 'vision statements', 'mission statements' or 'values' without them appearing trite, and I was anxious to avoid anything that smacked of management mantra. Written statements had to be reasonably general so as not to limit the scope of the company, but sufficiently specific to be meaningful. I had always tried to inculcate values that I believed in; I saw this, and a clear vision of the strategic direction of the business, as essential elements of leadership. So I spent considerable time working with Jo and Jane, who had consulted widely amongst staff, to create six statements which would encapsulate what LGC valued. A booklet and other material was produced for circulation to all staff and I launched this initiative myself in November 2002. In addressing staff at meetings throughout the Group, I tried to explain the principles and philosophy which I believed should underpin all LGC's activities, using some personal experiences to illustrate how drawing on held 'values' could guide decision-making. I was delighted that this exercise clearly struck a chord, particularly with younger staff, and I received very positive feedback from all levels in the organisation. Defining LGC's values is a legacy which I hope will last.

A related question associated with changing the culture of an organisation is how written rules and directives should be used and how far they should extend. With considerable care, Nicholas Clarke, a civil servant who had decided to stay with LGC after its privatisation and who was secretary of our board during our first few years and, for a time, was in charge of human resources, had overseen the production of a staff manual which set out all our rules of employment and provided guidance to managers on a range of issues, from disciplinary procedures to maternity/paternity leave. We had changed the arrangement for claiming business expenses and issued guidance on business hospitality and receiving gifts from customers and suppliers, and we had introduced new procedures in many areas. These rules and procedures, which had replaced a plethora of such rules which applied when LGC was part of the civil service, required thought and careful drafting. But a new topic was raised: should we introduce a dress code? Our business interactions now involved large numbers of customers and others visiting our laboratories and offices, and inevitably our visitors went away with impressions influenced, in some small part at least, by the appearance of staff. Should we therefore require our staff to dress reasonably smartly? There were those within the company who felt a dress code requiring sober smartness would help in promoting LGC's image; others felt a written dress code was going too far, and anyway it would be difficult to define what constituted reasonable dress. In regulating the conduct of a business – from assessment of risk to financial procedures to dress codes – it is tempting to produce more and more protocols and guidance documents. The problem is that the more written rules there are, the less they are read, and their purpose is lost. Even though all our rules and quality procedures were posted on the company intranet, many staff were blissfully unaware of their existence. In my view, however carefully they are drafted, written rules, though essential for financial or laboratory procedures, are not the way to influence attitudes and behaviour; it is quite often possible to adhere to the letter of a regulation while breaking its spirit by stretching it to the limit. The answer seems to me to lie in establishing a culture and a framework in which certain values and behaviour are the accepted norm, and where deviation from these is regarded as an abuse of trust. Creating such an organisational environment, which must extend from the top to the bottom, takes time, and it needs to be nurtured. Crass behaviour and breach of these norms, particularly by those at the top of an organisation, can rapidly destroy it.

On the business front, among the developments in 2002/3 were the establishment of a new DNA crime scene laboratory at Runcorn, in addition to our highly successful DNA laboratory at Teddington, and the formal opening, in September 2002, of our laboratory at Teddington dedicated for use by the Medicines and Healthcare products Regulatory Agency by the then Health Minister, Lord (Philip) Hunt, who cited this ten-year contract as a model public/private partnership for the provision of technical support services to government. On the scientific front, we invested further in our advanced mass spectroscopic expertise with the purchase of additional instrumentation to support our veterinary medicines and standards work. Moreover, the new Food Standards Agency, which had initially been slow to commission research work, started to call for proposals, and LGC was successful in winning a range of new work. LGC continued to be active within the analytical community and was the core partner in a new Faraday Partnership programme, supported by DTI and the Engineering and Physical Sciences Research Council, on High Throughput Technologies.

Our BSE testing contract was developing extremely well and we were managing to test increasing numbers of samples at our Teddington laboratory. However, the Food Standards Agency had recommended changes to the Over Thirty Month (OTM) Rule which prevented older cattle entering the food chain. In anticipation of this change, which would increase sample numbers considerably, we planned two new BSE testing laboratories in Runcorn and Edinburgh and they were opened in 2003. In fact, although Defra was keen to proceed with the new regime, the Department of Health held things up for a long time and ministerial decisions were delayed. Although the scientific case for a change in the regime for protecting the public had been thoroughly evaluated, the issue remained very sensitive. While decisions such as this should be based on evidence (and the independent scientific analysis by the Food Standards Agency was exemplary) public opinion has to be taken into account in any political decision. As a result of the government's delay in making a decision, the demand on our three BSE laboratories was initially much lower than planned, and it was some time before we were able to make the returns we had expected on these major investments.

The BSE programme proved to be interesting on the scientific front too. We had adopted a method of testing for the BSE agent, abnormal prions, which was incorporated in the so-called 'Enfer' test kits. However, other testing kits were being approved by the European Commission and we were approached by a US company, InPro, who wanted to evaluate their novel kit on real samples. InPro had been set up by Professor Stanley Prusiner of the University of California, San Francisco, and his colleague Jiri G. Safar. Stan Prusiner had won the Nobel prize for being the first to postulate the existence of prions, a new class of infectious agents thought to underlie a variety of neurodegenerative disorders. He and his team visited our Teddington laboratory where he gave a fascinating lecture on his work, and we agreed to evaluate InPro's new test kit. Following a number of reciprocal visits, including one I made to San Francisco with Ian Lumley (Head of our food division) and Ray Ah-Sun, during which we toured all the impressive facilities at the University for research on prion diseases, we signed a collaboration agreement with InPro which gave LGC European rights to the test kit. During a visit of his to London I arranged to take Professor Prusiner to meet Sir David King (the Government's Chief Scientific Adviser), Sir John Krebs (Chairman of the Food Standards Agency), Howard Dalton (Chief Scientist at Defra),

Lord May (President of the Royal Society), Ian Gibson MP (Chair of the House of Commons Select Committee on Science and Technology) and Professor Malcolm Grant (Chair of the Agriculture & Environment Biotechnology Commission). Professor Prusiner's argument that there should be much wider testing for prion diseases was listened to politely but, given that the US were virtually denying the existence of BSE and refused to undertake any testing, it was difficult for him to persuade UK policymakers that we were not doing enough. Moreover, I found it difficult to explain to a Nobel laureate that there were non-scientific issues, such as costs of materials and quality and reliability of supply, which influenced decisions on the choice of test to use. In the end, despite the fact that with LGC's help the InPro test had won approval from the European Commission, we decided to adopt another test system, manufactured by BioRad, for our future BSE testing programme. We were sad when InPro, having been sold to a major diagnostics company, Beckman Coulter, eventually had to close down. However, our work with Stan Prusiner and his team had deepened our understanding of testing for prion diseases. A programme which had begun as a testing service had developed a research component and had strengthened our science base.

In another part of LGC a technical issue was causing us increasing concern. Police forces took samples of DNA from suspects by asking them to swab the inside of their cheeks with a small felt pad attached to the end of a plastic stick. In our laboratories we extracted DNA from these felt pads, 'amplified' it (using a technique known as polymerase chain reaction or PCR) and then analysed the genetic pattern. If the final genetic pattern was not sufficiently clear, we would repeat the process. During 2002 we found that the 'failure rate' for analysis had increased and that we were having to repeat more and more of our work, a costly and time-consuming undertaking. Some of our customers were becoming irritated at an increase in our turnaround times, a critical measure which was closely monitored by police customers. Our most experienced staff investigated all parts of the process and concluded that the problem might lie with the felt pad. The DNA sampling kits were supplied by the Home Office Forensic Science Service (FSS) which occupied a curious position in the market. On the one hand they advised the government on forensic science matters and were required to audit and approve any new suppliers;

on the other hand, FSS was itself a supplier and competed strongly with newcomers such as LGC in offering services to the police. Not surprisingly, our relationship with FSS was uneasy. We felt they had delayed the introduction of our new Runcorn facility, costing us time and money, and when we then discovered that they had changed the supplier of the felt pads in the sampling kit without letting us know, we were, understandably, furious. I spoke to FSS's chief executive but he took no responsibility for the technical problems we were having with DNA extraction from the newly introduced swabs.

With the agreement of our board, I decided to take legal advice and consulted Simmons & Simmons, experts on commercial law. We fired the first gun by issuing a 'letter before action' claiming damages from FSS. Since they were responsible for swab specification and testing, they should have notified us before changing the supply of swabs. The matter dragged on for months before both sides finally agreed to avoid large legal costs by going to mediation, a non-adversarial procedure in which a neutral professional assists the parties in reaching settlement of a dispute. There were further delays before we agreed on the mediator from 'In Place of Strife' and the date for our meeting in February 2003.

The day arrived and, feeling apprehensive about how the dispute would be resolved, we met at the offices of Simmons and Simmons. We had already made written submissions and, briefed to the eyeballs by our legal and technical teams, I went in to bat with an aggressive opening statement arguing that FSS's behaviour was in breach of section 18 of the Competition Act 1988 and that this breach had resulted in LGC suffering loss. FSS responded by disclaiming any responsibility. The case revolved around some quite technical issues but the mediator immediately stated that he was not there to help resolve them. The implications of our competition case, on which we had sought Counsel's opinion, was that FSS was flouting competition law. Illustrating the difference between a government agency and a private company, FSS seemed, amazingly, to be relaxed about this possibly being referred to the Office of Fair Trading. The mediation involved shuttling between different rooms but it did not seem to achieve much. Late in the evening, when it was clear that we were getting nowhere, I decided to withdraw from further discussion. Up against an agency of a massive government department, it felt hugely frustrating, but the decision to withdraw paid off. Over the next few weeks there were exchanges between lawyers, and FSS clearly wanted to settle before reference to the courts. A meeting between our chairman, Ian Kent, and FSS's chairman, Rodger Pannone, helped to move things on and FSS finally offered to settle. The sum was less than the £1M+ we had sought, but it was still a good outcome. A more fundamental consequence, however, was that at last the Home Office recognised that there was a clear conflict between FSS's trading and custodian roles. Our action had highlighted the issue and accelerated the process to separate the two functions, an important achievement.

Meanwhile, after the initial integration problems had been resolved, our reference standards business, LGC Promochem, was performing strongly and we felt confident to explore a further acquisition, a small company called Mikromol, based at Lukenwald, a town in the Brandenburg region, 40km south of Berlin, which had particular expertise in the synthesis of pharmaceutical impurity reference standards. For several years Promochem (now LGC Promochem) had acted as their route to market, although Mikromol offered specialised services directly to customers. Mikromol had been founded in 1993 by Dr. Günter Funk and Dr. Hans Zimmermann, both highly able synthetic chemists who had developed a high quality and innovative company. As the company approached its tenth anniversary, the owners realised that it required new investment to grow further. LGC, already a close business partner, was an obvious home for the company. Mindful of our experience with the acquisition of Promochem, I again turned to Uwe de Buhr to act as an intermediary and, with Tilo Karrer and Ray Ah-Sun, we made slow but steady progress in agreeing terms for the sale. As with all small companies, it was quite difficult to conduct due diligence since the owners were deeply suspicious of being closely questioned. They had problems in appointing lawyers and final negotiations, which involved an earn-out, were protracted. However, I was also having difficulty in obtaining the full backing of LGC's board. Ray Ah-Sun and I tried to articulate a vision of a vertical integration of our reference standards production, but it was a difficult concept to get across and there were few hard figures to support the case. Not all board members were convinced and even my executive director colleagues had doubts. For Ray and me it was as much as anything a feeling in our bones that, with moves to generic brands, pharmaceutical impurities would become a major issue, and new reference standards would be required. The sale was not completed until June 2003 but we drew on our previous experience and moved quickly to integrate the business. In time, Mikromol proved to be one of our most successful acquisitions, repaying our investment many times over.

Within a short period of time, LGC had developed from a single site at Teddington into an international group with laboratories and offices in the UK, Germany, France, Spain, Poland and a joint venture in India. It was all the more important to exchange ideas and communicate both within and outside the company. I was fortunate in having an excellent PA, Lorna-Hopkinson Hall (who was a runner-up in The Times PA of the Year competition in 2004) who supported my commitment to communication. From the outset, we produced a staff newsletter, LGC News, which was sent to all staff and now covered news from all parts of the Group. As well as reporting company and business news, in short pieces from managers across the group, the newsletter also contained photographs and short biographies of new staff and often profiled a member of staff, recording their hobbies and interests as well as their professional achievements. With our monthly team briefing exercise and a new intranet, LGC News ensured that all staff throughout the Group in all the countries where we were now operating were kept up to date with developments in the company. More formally, we introduced a new consultative mechanism. In the UK a consultative committee consisting of elected staff representatives, union representatives, and managers discussed matters relating to terms and conditions of employment. A separate committee discussed health and safety matters. We also established an international consultative committee (a works council) where representatives of different sites would meet to discuss Group-wide issues. There are those who feel that works councils, based on the European model, are overly bureaucratic. I feel that it is vital for managers to listen to the views of staff representatives (trades union and other) and that open discussion of issues facing the company are important if changes are to be implemented smoothly. Our consultative structure, coupled with good two-way communications from our team briefing, helped establish good working relations throughout the company and there were very rarely any conflicts which were not resolved by formal or informal consultation.

With a strengthened board, impressive financial results under our belt, and very convincing prospects for growth in the pipeline, by 2003 we considered the timing was right for a transaction which would enable 3i to exit and for staff to realise at least some of the value of their shares. Although we had a very full agenda, we decided to launch Project Thaw, a major exercise to find a new investor.

Chapter 7: *Realising share-holder value*

Preparations for restructuring the Group – Bids from new investors – Professional award – Personal sorrow – LGV eventually replaces 3i as institutional investor

Preparation for the exit of 3i as our main shareholder had been going on in a quiet way for several years. Back in 2000 the board had commissioned Arthur Anderson to carry out a review of the company's development. Their report had not provided much new insight and, in feeding back as recommendations what the company was already doing, reinforced my prejudice that consultants often borrow your watch to tell you the time! During 2002 the board itself had reviewed the business and identified some 'non-core' activities which we felt could be shed. Although Pipeline Developments Ltd, the company that we had acquired in 1998, was itself doing well, it had not fulfilled the promise of providing a bridgehead for LGC into the water industry, and had never become fully integrated. Moreover, the privatised water industry no longer seemed such an attractive market for LGC and we wanted to focus our business development efforts on other areas with greater potential. We concluded that we should attempt to sell PDL and, with John Mason, now in charge of our northwest operations, taking the lead, we asked Paul Winson, whom I had first met on my mission to Japan, now at Trelawney Associates, to act for LGC in finding a new owner. After a well-managed sale process, PDL was sold to Bodycote in November 2002 for a price just a little more than we had paid nearly five years earlier.

Another non-core activity which we identified was our tobacco analysis business, which was based mainly on a long-standing contract with the Department of Health under which we carried out measurements of the tar and nicotine content of all types of cigarettes and other tobacco products. Our tobacco laboratory consisted of a series of impressive-looking smoking machines which puffed on cigarettes and captured their smoke. (For many years, lists of the tar and nicotine content of cigarette brands were on display in doctors' surgeries and referred to these measurements as being 'by the Government Chemist'.) We held discussions with Molins plc, an engineering company which manufactured equipment for cigarette production and packaging. They had recently acquired Battelle's tobacco testing business in the US from which they had created Arista Laboratories, and they were keen to set up a similar tobacco quality assurance laboratory in the UK. This seemed the perfect home and would, we hoped, provide a reasonably secure future for the ten or so staff involved. The Department of Health eventually agreed to transfer their contract to Arista and under an agreement, reached just before Christmas 2002, we continued to operate the laboratory until the work and staff could be moved to a laboratory which Arista set up in nearby Kingston-upon-Thames. It was sad to see the end of this work at LGC, since it had been the requirement for tobacco analysis which had led to the foundation of the Government Laboratory in 1842. However, we needed to look forward not back, and focus our management efforts on areas which we felt had the most growth and scientific potential.

Another matter to sort out was the position of the RSC. Totally unexpectedly and without any prior consultation, they had written to us to terminate their agreements with DTI and LGC covering the oversight of the Government Chemist function. Not only had they not acknowledged the huge financial return they had received from us the previous year, but they now did not even bother to telephone to discuss the implication for us of terminating agreements which it had taken their Working Party and Council months to agree back in 1996. Fortunately, DTI were not nearly as bothered as I had feared they might be and we subsequently managed to establish with DTI alternative arrangements for overseeing the Government Chemist. I will always be grateful for the support that RSC under Tom Inch gave to my management buy-out during 1995/6, but I confess that in the end I felt no regrets, rather a sense of relief, when the final links with the Society were severed.

More fundamentally, early in 2003 the board decided to appoint corporate finance advisers to assess LGC's value and to help find an appro-

In 2002, LGC Promochem delivered a wide range of reference materials from high specification storage facilities in the UK and Germany.

Achieving quality certification to ISO 9001 was an important move in our Polish office, led by Bolek Jerzac (centre).

A new purpose-built laboratory at Teddington processed over 36,000 samples during its first six months of operation and identified seven positive samples (none of which was destined to enter the food chain). Similar facilities were subsequently opened in Runcorn, Edinburgh and Exeter to support the health-protection programme put in place by the government.

An agreement with Professor Stanley Prusiner, whose biotech company Inpro developed a novel test method for prions (the agent causing BSE), gave LGC rights to validate the test and introduce it into Europe. Richard Worswick signs the agreement with Stanley Prusiner, watched by Scott McKinlay of Inpro.

My Entrepreneur of the Year Award in 2003 marked LGC's success.

When Baroness James of Holland Park, the crime writer P D James, opened our new forensic DNA laboratory at Runcorn she noted that: 'Science has made such astonishing advances that we're in danger of writing novels with very swift endings. None of us can ever again permit our murderer to leave behind the sort of blood-stained handkerchief Agatha Christie was so fond of!'

The board of LGC Group Holdings plc in 2005. From left: Uwe de Buhr (non-executive), Joanne Parfrey (non-executive representing LGV), Geoff Battersby (group finance director), Richard Worswick (deputy chairman), Nigel Law (chief executive), Lord Stevens (non-executive), Ian Kent (chairman), Brian Phillips (non-executive representing LGV), John Mason (director, corporate development).

Ian Lumley, Head of Food Chain and Environment, and Peter Farnell, Head of Food Chain Analysis, assess the performance of new methods for the determination of functional ingredients in foods.

LGC has sales offices across India. The laboratory for the manufacture of reference materials is in Bangalore. Here Sury Rao (seated right) and the initial laboratory team are joined by Hans Zimmermann, from LGC's Berlin laboratory, (seated 2nd from left) who provided training in some specialist aspects of chemical synthesis.

Ray Ah-Sun, Derek Craston and Sury Rao, three key players in LGC's development, discuss plans for expansion in India and the Far East.

Our restaurant, Helix, proved very popular amongst staff at Teddington and provided a place for informal and business meetings.

The annual charity chosen by staff provided a focus for fundraising and social occasions. Here my successor as chief executive, David Richardson, presents a cheque to actor Kevin Whately for Alzheimer's Society.

priate way for 3i to exit and for staff shareholders, of whom there were now over 400 of our total staff of 600, to realise at least some of the value of their shares. We wanted to complete the process as quickly as possible so as to minimise any disruption to the business. At the time we were not only making an acquisition (of Mikromol) in Germany but were about to open a new office in Italy. We approached six firms and shortlisted three, who gave presentations to the board.

Choosing an adviser often seems to me to come down to gut feeling. Most of the big firms quote similar charges and have similar models for valuing businesses. However, all our board liked the straightforward approach and absence of arrogance of the Deloitte and Touche team which was led by Marc Gillespie and, after Clive Hall had engaged in tough negotiations of terms, they were appointed at the end of March 2003. They began work immediately on an information memorandum and Clive Hall prepared a three-year management forecast, the first year of which was our recently completed budget. With major contributions from me and my colleagues, the first draft of the IM was completed by the end of May and looked impressive. In the meantime, Marc and his team had contacted several potential trade buyers and, since rumour travels amazingly swiftly in the corporate finance community, Deloitte had already been approached by a long list of private equity groups who had followed our progress and were aware of our success and were keenly interested in acquiring our very attractive company.

On Deloitte's advice, the board had decided to appoint Pricewaterhouse-Coopers (PwC) to undertake 'vendor due diligence', the purpose of which was to provide potential buyers with an independent report on all aspects – legal, commercial and financial – of the business and so avoid the disruption caused by vendors each conducting their own due diligence. Potential bidders were given just six weeks to submit indicative offers and during July the management team gave a series of corporate presentations. These presentations were carefully choreographed and began in the afternoon. I gave an overview of the development of the business which emphasised its unique and robust nature, the experienced management team, and LGC's high growth and low risk potential. John Mason talked about the staff and culture of the organisation, highlighting what had been achieved through the Pentagon Programme. Nigel

Law gave details of the business, going through the activities of each division and identifying some of the many opportunities for growth. Clive Hall reviewed LGC's outstanding record of continuous growth and then outlined the financial forecasts, listing a number of major tenders which we would be pursuing over the coming year. At the end of the presentation I felt extremely proud of what had been achieved over the previous seven years and that the company I had created was such a dynamic organisation, full of potential. At the end of each presentation we were joined by Ray Ah-Sun, John Marriott and Jo Bloomfield for further discussions and we then took our potential new investors to an early dinner at the nearby Petersham Hotel where they were able to cross-question the wider team and to outline their plans for the future.

It rapidly became apparent that the most serious (and highest) bidders were private equity groups. To me, this defied logic since trade buyers might be expected to put a premium on 'strategic fit'. It also raised some fundamental issues. Whereas a trade buyer would consider how to fit the management of LGC within their own operations (and I had some separate discussions with some of the bidders along these lines, including a visit to Barcelona to meet with one of them), a private equity buyer would normally expect the backing of the current management team. Of the three we selected from those who had submitted final bids by the beginning of August, two were private equity firms. The transaction was therefore likely to become a 'secondary buy-out', a refinancing of the business but not an exit of the management shareholders.

This had different implications for different members of the senior management team. Nigel and Clive were both ambitious and eager to become chief executive. However, neither were entrepreneurs in the sense that they wanted to take the initiative in putting forward their own proposals. John Mason, now living in Cheshire, was not sure that he would remain at LGC for the rest of his career. My motivation was very different. Our eldest daughter Helen, who had been ill for many years, was now very frail and the burden of caring for her, which for years had fallen particularly on my wife Jacqueline, had become very heavy for us both. I wanted to see a secure future for the company I had worked so hard to create, but I also wanted the prospect of being able to stand down as chief executive so that I could have more time with Jacquie and with our daughters. Jacquie and I were both tired and drained after years of caring day and night for Helen, and needed more time.

In the final round, the offers from private equity companies were significantly higher than those from the trade bidders. Since financial investors use similar models for valuing companies, there was relatively little difference between the private equity offers, and choosing between them was therefore mainly a question of who the management team could best work with in the future. There was also the issue of how much of the proceeds from the sale of their shares the management and staff would be required to reinvest in the new company. Two private equity bidders stood out – Close Brothers and Legal & General Ventures – mainly because we liked the people who were leading their teams. In the end we selected Legal & General Ventures who seemed to have connected well with our business. Their bid required substantial reinvestment by senior management but would allow most staff to sell their shares and, and although I would be required to 'roll over' the same amount as four other senior managers, I would be able to sell sufficient shares to become financially independent.

The LGV team was led by a sharp and amusing Glaswegian, Brian Phillips, who was particularly interested in the forensics side of LGC's business. Despite the fact that PwC had prepared a full vendor due diligence report, as soon as we had entered a period of exclusive negotiations, Brian and his assistant, Jo Parfrey, got down to commissioning a fair amount of their own due diligence – environmental reports, business due diligence, and psychometric tests and interviews of the senior team. The process confirmed my prejudice that venture capitalists are hugely rewarded for investing other people's money, but they protect their backsides with dozens of expensive reports commissioned from 'experts'.

Brian came to Germany to visit LGC Promochem's operations in Wesel and our newly acquired company, Mikromol, near Berlin, and met senior representatives of USP, a key supplier of pharmaceutical reference materials, who assured him of the solidity of their relationship with LGC. Brian had lined up two banks – Bank of Ireland and Société Générale. Having had an excellent relationship with HSBC since my initial buyout, I was keen that they should also be part of the consortium providing debt finance. Brian agreed to this, and meetings and presentations were arranged with the three banks. Our lawyers, Eversheds, started to pre-pare documentation with LGV's lawyers, Camerons.

Not everything went smoothly, however. It transpired that LGV had retained PwC as their advisers. LGC's board, particularly our chairman, Ian Kent, felt that PwC had a conflict of interest in acting for LGC, the seller, in conducting vendor due diligence, and at the same time giving advice to LGV, the buyer. What incensed us was the complacent reaction of PwC when Ian raised the matter. The issue rapidly escalated into a row which threatened to derail the whole process. Brian understood PwC's argument that there were 'Chinese walls' between different parts of their organisation but Ian felt that the 'Chinese walls' were flimsy and, at the very least, we should have been informed formally of a potential conflict of interest. I was desperate to cool things and arranged to see PwC's compliance director, but that seemed only to inflame things further. He was extremely arrogant and implied that PwC was such an important firm that LGC's concern about ethical behaviour on what he clearly regarded as a minor deal was a matter which was beneath him. There were only two ways the issue could be settled: either we pulled out of the deal or we reached a compromise. I had discussions on my own with LGV's contact at PwC and arranged for him to reduce his fees by £100K without prejudice but in quiet recognition of the poor way LGC had been treated and in desperation to unlock the situation. Thank goodness the board accepted this compromise.

A more significant hiccup related to clearance of the transaction by the tax authorities, and the important question of how much tax would be payable by staff and management shareholders who were 'rolling over' their proceeds into the 'new' company. An application by Eversheds was met (after the statutory 28 days) with a response which was difficult to fathom. There seemed to be no opportunity to engage in dialogue with Inland Revenue. Frustrated by the delays, we asked the tax department at Deloitte and Touche to intervene and eventually a meeting was arranged with an official from HM Revenue & Customs. At this meeting the Revenue proposed a deal under which they would agree to drop their objection to the tax levied on the staff shareholders intending to re-invest in the 'new' company, in exchange for an apparently arbitrarily calculated levy on the company. This was an unexpected and, frankly, bizarre proposal, not based on tax regulation but simply on the arbitrary opinion of an official. However, we were effectively forced to accept it to enable the transaction to go ahead.

Negotiating with bidders, giving presentations to banks, and ploughing through interminable legal agreements was fairly relentless, but we were still focused on what could be achieved in the future. Meanwhile, what had already been achieved in the past was being evaluated by the judges of the Entrepreneur of the Year contest run by Ernst & Young, in association with The Times. The competition had begun at the beginning of 2003 and, after interviews and a visit by the assessment team, I had reached the regional finals and gone on to win an award for the London region. An advertisement in the Financial Times by one of the sponsors of the Award, Hennessy Cognac, praised my 'entrepreneurial spirit' (!) in transforming a government agency into a successful science-based service company. Winning a regional award meant that my name went forward to the national finals, culminating in a lavish dinner and award ceremony at the Grosvenor Hotel in Park Lane. Jacquie and I had been to the regional awards event on our own, but this time I invited my close colleague Ray Ah-Sun and his wife and Brian Phillips, managing director of Legal & General Ventures, and his wife. We were joined by colleagues from HSBC, the bank which had supported my management buy-out and with which LGC had excellent relations.

I really was not expecting to win the national award but, unlike at the regional finals, this time I had prepared a few words just in case. I was amazed when, after the short films on each of the finalists in the products and services category, my name was taken from the envelope and I was called to the stage to receive the award. After thanking my colleagues and Jacquie, I told a short joke which fortunately went down well (and was later quoted in The Times and recycled at the awards ceremony the following year by the presenter, Jeremy Vine). As I returned to our table clutching a curious wooden and metal object (the competition's take on the Oscar trophy) on which my name was engraved, Jacquie turned to Brian who was still negotiating with us over the purchase of LGC and said: 'The price has just gone up!' The excitement and spirit of goodwill generated by the award certainly helped over the turbulent weeks that followed.

Another very enjoyable event during the seemingly relentless grind of Project Thaw was the opening of LGC's new forensic laboratories at Runcorn. The expansion of our forensic business had been a great success story and our investment in new facilities at Runcorn reflected our confidence in this area of our business. The Commissioner of the Metropolitan Police had formally opened our DNA facilities at Teddington in May 1998 and we had considered inviting a Home Office minister or chief constable to open our Runcorn laboratory. However, Jacquie suggested that it would be much more interesting to invite the crime writer P D James, whom she had got to know through a BBC committee, and I was very pleased when she agreed to perform this task. Baroness James's visit to Runcorn was a delightful occasion. Drawing on her experiences at the Home Office and as a crime writer, she gave a thoughtful and stimulating speech on the importance of an understanding of science and science education. She seemed so interested in everyone she met and everything she saw during her tour of the laboratories. Her visit generated considerable interest and was covered on the regional television network. A photograph of her with a lethal weapon which our forensic scientists were examining appeared in several of the national newspapers.

LGC's senior management team were required to sign warranties (confirming that the information we had supplied to Legal & General Ventures was accurate) and I spent time quizzing them and Clive Hall about achieving our budget forecast. A particular issue related to the level of BSE testing. Anticipating the change in the Over Thirty Month (OTM) scheme, we had recruited new staff and opened new laboratories, but the ministerial decision had still not been taken. Nevertheless, the business seemed to be performing according to budget. LGV's actual offer was agreed at a tense meeting between Andrew Fraser of 3i, Brian Phillips, Ian Kent and me. Although LGV adhered to their initial bid, there were various adjustments to be agreed, including for fees. Andrew was surprisingly reluctant to agree the offer and the meeting was far from straightforward, but Ian exercised considerable diplomacy in shuttling between the two parties and finally persuading Andrew to accept a deal which, after all, would deliver a profit to 3i of around £20 million. This translated into an offer of £19. 10 per share.

However, there were further delays, this time with getting the banking documentation sorted out, and it wasn't until just before Christmas that we were in a position to send offer letters to shareholders. On Monday 22nd December at a meeting of all staff at Teddington in the Helix restaurant (the only room big enough to accommodate everyone, even standing) I explained that LGC was about to change its share structure and that Legal & General Ventures would be replacing 3i as the institutional shareholder. I announced the offer price and explained with examples what this would mean for staff shareholders. Although new ownership was an important change, it would be 'business as usual'; there would be changes to our board, but there would be no changes to our management team and we would continue to strive to serve our customers, to develop our science and to build our business.

I had kept staff informed of the process as it progressed, but the actual terms came as a complete surprise to most of those present. The following day letters were dispatched to all shareholders and share option holders. Sending out the letters was a complex logistical operation and the previous evening, Nigel Law and I had joined a dedicated small band of assistants in stuffing over 400 envelopes with sets of documents which varied according to the particular circumstances of the shareholder. About 50 staff were asked to 'roll over' some of the proceeds from the sale of their shares into the new company and, to help all staff to understand the offer, information and a question and answer briefing were circulated. We also provided some excellent material on how to deal with a financial windfall. I went home for the Christmas break exhausted by the process that had led to this point, but relieved that a route had now opened to my eventual exit from the company.

However, Jacquie and I soon had much more important matters on our mind. Our daughter Helen had developed a chest infection on her birthday (on which I always took a day's holiday), just a week before Christmas. Despite her frailty, Helen had shaken off similar infections before. There had been previous occasions when she had seemed critically ill, but had somehow pulled through. We nursed her over Christmas when we were joined by her sisters, Catherine and Isobel. Helen's GP, who had been involved with us in the foundation of Helen House, called in every couple of days and prescribed medicines to ease her discomfort. Helen's condition seemed to stabilise but I went to my office at Teddington, closed between Christmas and the New Year, to tidy my desk and to leave a message for my director colleagues warning them that I might not be able to return immediately in the New Year. Whenever I now hear the music I listened to in the car, on my journey to and from Teddington, a CD that we often played to Helen, I recall my desperate sadness during the days immediately after Christmas. Helen was very frail and unable to be fed and was pathetically pale. She somehow managed to swallow small quantities of liquid, but she slept for much of the time. She died on the afternoon of 4th January, listening as always to beautiful music, and with her family.

We arranged for Helen's funeral to take place on Saturday 10th January, in the small village church where Jacquie and I had been married. Jacquie remained remarkably in control and read a beautiful poem by Thomas Hardy and she and Catherine delivered very moving tributes to our beloved daughter. I managed to get through the funeral service and the burial that followed before returning home distraught. Helen's birth in 1975 had brought such happiness to Jacquie and me, and for nearly three years our lives were devoted to our bright and sunny little daughter. These short years of undiluted joy, and the subsequent arrival of her wonderful sisters, sustained us through the long years of looking after our very sick daughter. Although we might be thought to have had many years to prepare ourselves, her death was nevertheless a terrible shock and we felt totally bereft. The grief of losing our well little child 25 years earlier welled up again and was combined with the grief of losing the brave child and young person we had nursed and loved for so long. For me, returning to work just days after her funeral, was a temporary escape from a sadness which has never lifted.

On my return to work I was greeted with great kindness but a major problem. Clive Hall, our finance director, had taken a long holiday over Christmas to attend a friend's wedding in New Zealand and, when he returned, he found that our trading figures were substantially below the forecast on which LGV's offer had been based. His view was that we should not draw attention to this, but I felt that as a matter of principle we should be totally open about our trading performance. Clive and I disagreed fundamentally; but, after consulting other colleagues, including our chairman, I decided I had no choice but to go to LGV to brief them on the situation. Brian Phillips agreed that the current offer, which was now with all staff shareholders, should be put on hold. I immediately informed staff that the Extraordinary General Meeting of shareholders, which would have completed the sale process, was to be postponed. It seemed to me that the only way we could recover from this situation was to re-work all our forecasts, division by division, and I asked my trusted colleague John Mason, with the assistance of Deloitte, to undertake this task. We agreed not to rush this process and for the next three weeks John Mason went through the financial estimates and forecasts of each division. With great patience and working long into every evening, he interrogated the heads of divisions and their staff and assembled new forecasts based on a detailed and painstaking analysis.

Several of the senior management team were at fault in failing to spot the deviation from our profit forecasts, which it now appeared had begun several months earlier, but it was particularly humiliating for Clive to see John Mason pick apart his rather broad brush and, it transpired, erroneous forecasts. (In many ways it was fortunate that Clive went on sick leave to deal with a longstanding medical complaint and did not take part in this process.) In my view, it was also an indictment of the due diligence process. Enormous fees were paid for a due diligence report which had fully endorsed all the previous forecasts. This incident did nothing to enhance the reputation of management consultants. By mid February 2004 the revised forecasts, lower than those prepared the previous summer, were completed. PwC re-worked their due diligence and, for a second time (this time correctly), agreed with our forecasts. The figures were also crawled over by Ernst & Young, our auditors.

There followed a series of meetings with LGV and the three banks and, finally, the negotiation of a revised offer with Brian Phillips. LGV could so easily have taken unfair advantage of the situation but Brian had attended a meeting of LGC's board in January and assured us of his confidence that LGC remained a very strong and attractive business. LGV put forward two options for a revised offer, one involving a reduction in the share price, the other involving an earn-out and deferred payments. The board considered the simpler option of a reduced share price of £16.70 per share the more favourable for the majority of shareholders.

However, from a personal point of view there was a very significant new condition attached to the offer; I would be required to remain as chief executive for at least a year and then to remain on the board. Moreover, I would not be able to sell the majority of my shares but would be required to 'roll over' twice as much as I had wanted. In some ways it was flattering to be regarded as such a vital asset, but the outcome was not what I had hoped. I had intended to pave the way for my exit from the company I had founded; I was now being tied tightly to the ship's mast. Despite representations by Ian Kent on my behalf, I realised that I had no choice but to agree to these new conditions to ensure the transaction went ahead. It was hoped that final agreement from the three banks, HSBC, Bank of Ireland, and Société Générale, who together were providing £30 million of debt, might be forthcoming to allow the transaction to proceed before the end of the financial year. However, their agreement delayed until 7 April the issue of the new offer to shareholders which was approved at an EGM (extraordinary general meeting) on 28 April and declared unconditional the following day.

The structure of the new company was quite complicated. LGV and about 50 managers and staff purchased approximately 1,000,000 £1 shares and £9 million of unsecured loan notes in a new holding company, LGC Group Holdings plc. A subsidiary company, LGC Investments Limited, together with the holding company, had a £35 million credit agreement with the three banks, of which £30 million was a term loan and £5 million was a working capital facility. LGC Investments Limited purchased the entire share capital of LGC (Holdings) Ltd, the company I had founded in 1996 as the vehicle for the purchase of the Laboratory of the Government Chemist. The consideration paid was approximately £59 million, but this was after the payment of a vast sum (approximately £5 million) for the fees of the various advisers and lawyers. What a contrast with the fees I had paid (less than £200,000) in the transaction 8 years earlier! Although I have great respect for good lawyers, accountants, actuaries etc, I resent the fact that they are rarely accountable for the advice they give and that their fees associated with transactions are frequently exorbitant.

With the change of ownership of LGC, Dennis Stocks and Marion Sears resigned as non-executive directors of our board. I was delighted that Ian Kent was re-appointed non-executive chairman and that John

Beacham agreed to stay on the board for a further year. LGV recommended that Geoff Battersby, an experienced accountant, should advise the company on its financial systems, and Clive Hall agreed to leave the company. Geoff was subsequently appointed Group Finance Director.

I received many appreciative and touching letters of gratitude from members of staff, who told me how the windfall they had received from the sale of their shares had affected their lives. These letters included one from the mother of a junior assistant whom, without I hope breaching financial regulations, I had coaxed into exercising the option she had been given to purchase shares. The £16,000 windfall she received, the minimum received by staff who had been present when the company was formed in 1996, had made a real difference to their family. Some staff, who had purchased shares received as much as several hundred thousand pounds. Most staff took the advice which we gave not to go out and spend all their windfall at once (which averaged £32,000 for each of the 400 or so shareholder staff) and, rather to my surprise, only two staff decided to leave to pursue other interests.

So, by the end of the first quarter of 2004/5, LGC was able to focus again on its business and I was still fixed in the driving seat. Although we had a new board, it was in many ways business as usual, working hard to fulfil the plans set out in our information memorandum the year before and to expand LGC geographically and develop new areas of business.

Chapter 8: *Building for the future*

Board changes – Plans for further growth – International expansion – Handing over to a new chief executive and becoming deputy chairman – Opportunities in forensic science – Problems with acquisition and integration – Changes at LGV – A new chairman and chief executive – Handing over the reins for a second time – Reflections on creating an international company

Over the years when 3i was our institutional investor, and as our reputation grew, I had been invited to an increasing number of events and award ceremonies organised by banks and private equity companies who had become aware of LGC and its success and were interested in its future. These events often provided interesting opportunities to meet others who had founded and developed successful businesses. I recall a dinner organised by Hg Capital at which Paul Pindar, who with its founder, Rod Aldridge, had built Capita within 20 years from a company with two employees in the mid 1980s into a highly successful outsourcing company with a £billion turnover, described how this had been achieved. He said that the most challenging period had been growing turnover from £1m to £50m. Thereafter, the company had the resources to establish proper infrastructure and it was sufficiently robust to face the occasional setback.

As it turned out, what I experienced at LGC was similar. Achieving the £50m turnover milestone had been enormously demanding; for years I had worked incredibly hard and almost without a break. With the death of our eldest daughter I had wanted to stand down, but LGC's new investor, Legal & General Ventures, had insisted that I continue at the helm to lead the company to further success. Although this was not what I had planned, I was confident that the next phase in LGC's development would be easier and I was hopeful that I would be able to delegate more tasks, especially if I could strengthen our senior management.

After the refinancing of the company and LGV becoming the majority shareholder, our board had changed. Ian Kent continued as chairman and John Beacham continued as a non-executive but, Dennis Stocks and Marion Sears having stepped down, they were joined by Brian Phillips and his assistant Jo Parfrey from LGV. The executive members of the board were me, Nigel Law, John Mason and Geoff Battersby, the interim finance director who had stood in to replace Clive Hall.

Having always believed in the value of strong independent non-executive directors, I suggested that our board could usefully be strengthened by people with international and forensic experience. Uwe de Buhr, with whom I had worked closely on our acquisition of Promochem and who had played a pivotal advisory role in our acquisition of Mikromol, agreed to join the board in December 2004, and I wrote to Sir John Stevens inviting him to join our board on his retirement early in 2005 from being Commissioner of the Metropolitan Police. Ian Kent and I 'interviewed' him at Teddington. John Stevens's energy and enthusiasm were engaging. It was clear that he and I had rather different views on some topics; he is a staunch monarchist and was delighted to be joining the House of Lords, whereas I had always supported constitutional reform, including abolishing the current honours system and reforming the second chamber. However, we shared views on the importance of forensic science and the advantages of an independent provider such as LGC working alongside the dominant government-owned agency, the Forensic Science Service. Ian and I were pleased when Sir John (soon to become Lord) Stevens, agreed to join a board which was working well together. He replaced John Beacham, who stood down in March 2005, having been a great support and having helped see LGC through many changes, including changes of investors.

While on the board, John Beacham had not only chaired our remuneration committee but had also had the onerous task of chairing our pension fund trustees. Ian Kent suggested that we should look for a new chairman for our pension scheme from outside the company and introduced me to James Cook, a retired corporate financier who had taken a particular interest in pension funds and was already a trustee of several company schemes. When I met him I was immediately impressed by Jim's grasp of the issues facing our pension fund, still managed at the time by Scottish Widows, and I felt that he would be a great help to the other trustees. With their agreement, he was appointed and over subsequent years made a vital contribution to sorting out the problems which arose continually during that period with almost all company pension schemes. Jim is an amateur musician and an unexpected pleasure arising from his appointment was the opportunity for me to play the violin accompanied by him on the piano and, on one occasion in Kingston Parish Church, the organ. (He introduced me to some sonatas by Rheinberger for violin and organ which I had not come across before.)

At the board's first strategy meeting, held at the nearby Petersham Hotel a few weeks after the LGV transaction, we had agreed plans to reinforce our senior management team and to shift the focus of the organisation further towards our markets and customers and away from being centred on the underpinning technology. We began the long process of finding and appointing staff to fill some key positions which led, in particular, to the appointment of John McQuillian to head our life sciences business and Matthias Brommer to head our standards business. Piece by piece we were able to strengthen our management at all levels and the effects of this were felt with the growth of the business. The selection of senior managers is crucial to the success of a business. The management team I chose to create was not a collection of clones with identical approaches; rather, I wanted to assemble leaders with different skills and different approaches to tackling problems. Managing heterogeneous teams sometimes presents problems and there needs to be mutual respect and understanding if such teams are to work effectively. I always involved colleagues in the selection of candidates for senior management positions, since we would all have to work together once a new person had been appointed.

After the problems encountered during the prolonged sale of the company and the moderation of our business forecasts, our business bounced back during 2004/5. The new BSE testing regime was at last introduced by Defra and the new state-of-the-art laboratories we had planned and commissioned at Runcorn and in Edinburgh, for which we had recruited and trained staff who would work into the evening and sometimes overnight, ran like clockwork and generated good financial returns. Growth in our forensic services, our reference standards business and scrapie genotyping, and the early success of our new acquisition, Mikromol, all contributed to excellent results for 2005 which were well ahead of our forecasts.

LGC was now established as an international group. Most of our operations were in Europe and it was our policy to appoint nationals as country managers because they would be fully cognisant with their country's culture and business practice. This may appear strange in a single European market, but there are distinctly different regulations and procedures in different countries, for example for the import and export of pharmaceutical and biological products. The offices in the different countries we operated in were staffed predominantly by well-qualified and experienced people who could speak to customers fluently in their own language and were knowledgeable about their requirements. Some of the offices we acquired from Promochem had minority share interests, but over time we reached agreements to ensure that LGC (or one of the subsidiaries of our holding company) acquired 100% of the shares. There were also issues around directorships which had to be resolved; several of our subsidiary companies were required by law to have non-UK nationals as directors so, in addition to the local managing director (who was always a non-UK national), LGC's non-executive director, Uwe de Buhr, took on a number of additional responsibilities.

As our European business developed, we gradually improved our operational logistics. Physical stocks of reference materials were kept in Wesel, where there were purpose-built storage facilities, and at Teddington, although smaller country offices maintained modest stocks of key items. Although customers initially liked to have physical catalogues of the materials we supplied, and faxed through their orders, we gradually shifted to web catalogues and internet sales. In this context, it is worth noting that the internet has allowed even quite small companies to penetrate international markets at relatively low cost. However, although LGC invested heavily in the information systems to support our standards business, there is often no substitute for a sales person familiar with the needs, regulatory requirements and language of their customers.

Our joint venture operation in India was rather different. This was a

50/50 joint venture which was managed by our co-owner, Sury Rao, an experienced and highly entrepreneurial business man, with whom Ray Ah-Sun and I worked closely. Sury set up a network of regional offices which were serviced by high-quality staff; later, in conjunction with Derek Craston (by now a senior scientist at Teddington) and scientists from Lukenwalde (Mikromol), he planned and set up impressive laboratory facilities in Bangalore. It was in connection with the planning of this new laboratory that I first met Sury's guru. Ray and I had been awaiting Sury's arrival from Heathrow airport for a meeting at Teddington when the receptionist telephoned us to say that he was in reception and unexpectedly was accompanied by a 'priest'. Ray had met Sury's spiritual guru on a previous occasion and quickly gave me advice on how to handle the formalities of the meeting. Our introduction went well and LGC seemed to pass the first test of being an ethical organisation with which to do business. Sury placed a lot of faith in the judgement of his guru, and I rapidly understood why. Mostly the guru listened to our discussions, but his occasional interjections were clearly based on considerable experience of business. The advice he gave in relation to the new laboratory we were planning in Bangalore– to lease a building rather than, as Sury had initially favoured, build a new laboratory on a greenfield site – turned out to be very wise. Although dealing with a 'priest' was strange for someone used to Western ways of business, I developed a respect for the thoughtful and even spiritual component to doing business in India. The relationship between Sury and Ray was not always easy but they both had an instinct for new business opportunities, and our Indian company went from strength to strength.

We spent some time considering the language and cultural implications of our international development. Our inter-company communications were in English, but it was important that staff should be aware of behavioural differences that could give rise to misunderstandings, and that they should respect each other's cultures. I was struck by the huge differences there were. On one visit to Sweden I was informed that the country manager, who had only just been appointed and whom I was expecting to meet, was absent because he was taking several weeks' paternity leave. By contrast, meetings with managers in India sometimes continued long into the night and over weekends. My six-monthly talks to staff, which were simple to organise in the UK, now involved travelling to all offices, so we divided the task between our executive management team. I enjoyed the opportunity to meet staff at all levels during trips to Warsaw, Borås, Milan or Bangalore and I never ceased to be proud in visiting our far-flung offices to see the LGC logo (with my wife's strapline, 'Settting standards in analytical science') attached to buildings in such very different locations. Our 'country managers' also met every six months or so, and we decided that the place of the meeting should rotate between our various offices. After our formal meeting there would often be a social event. The imagination and ingenuity displayed by the organisers of these events in the host country, who clearly wanted to give their colleagues from overseas a taste of their culture, generated tremendous goodwill. At one such event that I attended in Teddington, I reflected that playing skittles on a summer's evening soon broke down barriers between the various nations represented and dispelled undue formality.

I was keen that more able staff from our different operations overseas should attend our Ashridge management training programme, and up-and-coming managers from France, Germany, Poland and India came to the UK to do so, partly to enhance their skills but also to strengthen our corporate unity. A number of staff were involved in exchanges and secondments for longer periods. All of this helped to create a cohesive and almost family spirit in LGC.

After the distraction of the refinancing, the company was once again firing on all cylinders and I was pleased to be focusing on developing our business further. However, our daughter Helen's death had affected Jacquie and me very deeply. During Helen's long illness we had in theory had years to prepare ourselves, but we had not anticipated the devastating effect her death would have on our family. We felt exhausted and bereft. I took a month off during the autumn; we went to Cyprus for some sun and spent some time in Cornwall where I had some intensive violin lessons. However, we both found it difficult adjusting to life without our eldest daughter whom we had cared for for so many years. With the agreement of LGV, I stood down as chief executive in March 2005 and became deputy chairman, in principle working three days a week and responsible for the strategic development of the LGC Group. I was very pleased to hand over to Nigel Law whom I liked and with whom I worked well.

Unbeknown to me, in the autumn of 2003 my name had been put forward for an honour and in May 2004 I received a letter from the Secretary for Appointments at 10 Downing Street. Having always been critical of the honours system, I felt it would be hypocritical to accept, even if in declining I would disappoint the people who had made submissions on my behalf. In my brief reply, I explained why I felt the honours system was discredited and my disappointment that the government had not tackled constitutional reform. I also noted the uncomfortably backward-looking connotations of the title 'Commander of the Order of the British Empire'. I received a polite letter in reply saying that my points would be taken into account in any future review of the honours system. Some will understand my position; others will no doubt regard it as eccentric or even disloyal. However, in my view it is possible to be patriotic and at the same time argue for fundamental constitutional change. In this context, I find it extraordinary that the Prime Minister can effectively choose and appoint large numbers of people to become members of our second chamber, unelected but part of our legislature. Such patronage would be (indeed is) roundly condemned in other regimes. Returning to the honours system, I do realise the pleasure that reward through this system can bring, and have been pleased when the dedication of people who have worked selflessly and often for modest reward (such as the first head nurse at Helen House) has been publicly recognised in this way.

Our new strategic plan had identified forensic science as a major opportunity for growth. My own involvement with forensic science had begun ten years earlier when, as Government Chemist, I had been asked to give evidence to the House of Lords Select Committee (rather an impressive group incidentally, which, though unelected, included many eminent scientists!) which was investigating the subject in the aftermath of miscarriages of justice which had arisen from erroneous forensic evidence. With Ric Treble, then head of our drugs team at LGC, I had appeared before the committee, chaired by Lord Dainton, and had argued that forensic science was not *per se* a scientific discipline; rather, it drew on a collection of different scientific disciplines. I had discussed the difficulty of expressing measurement uncertainty in front of a court which wanted complete certainty – the word 'uncertainty', a standard term in analytical measurement, would immediately undermine the evidence presented – and I had described the approach to ensuring the quality of analytical measurements which was being pursued through the DTI's valid Analytical Measurement Programme which LGC managed. I had subsequently invited Lord (Fred) Dainton to LGC and had been invited by Lord (Jack) Lewis to join a small group examining ways of ensuring standards among forensic practitioners. With Home Office support this led to the creation of The Council for the Registration of Forensic Practitioners (CRFP) of which I was invited to become a founding member. The Council began well under the chairmanship of Professor Evelyn Ebsworth (formerly Vice Chancellor of Durham University) but sadly was wound up a few years later after the withdrawal of Home Office funding. I had also gained a considerable understanding of the particular features of forensic evidence while working with Police Forces to establish LGC's DNA laboratory, back in 1996.

Up to this point LGC had concentrated on forensic measurements which could be made in the laboratory – drugs analysis, DNA profiling, trace metal detection, etc – and, with the exception of our long-standing and highly-respected questioned documents team, had generally avoided those areas of forensic science which related to interpretation of evidence, particularly at the scene of crime. This was a deliberate policy. While I was confident that LGC had quality systems and procedures covering our laboratory measurements – we were the first 'forensic laboratory' in the UK to be accredited – I was less confident about systems for ensuring the integrity of opinions formed, and measurements made, at the actual scene of a crime. I had by now met many forensic scientists, among whom were a few who appeared arrogant and too sure of their own judgement. Anyone could claim to be an expert and it was difficult for a court to know the background and expertise of someone parading as an 'expert witness' and offering opinion evidence. It was for this reason that I had strongly supported the idea of a Register of Forensic Practitioners, although the practicality of overseeing this register ultimately proved too difficult. However, there was no doubt that science was a powerful and increasingly important tool in the investigation of crime and there was considerable merit in highly professional companies such as LGC, as well as the Home Office Forensic Science Service, providing services to the police. The expansion in the use of forensic science, and the gradual opening up to competition of services required by police forces, provided an excellent opportunity for LGC to develop a more comprehensive service.

We examined opportunities within and outside the UK. We knew the players in the UK well and several years earlier had attempted to acquire Cellmark, a small independent provider of DNA services, from its then owner, Zeneca. We had also had contact with Forensic Alliance Ltd, a consultancy which had been set up by Dr Angela Gallop, an experienced and respected forensic scientist who had formerly worked for the Forensic Science Service, and her husband. Forensic Alliance was quite complicated in that it was based on several 'alliances' with specialist providers, including Cellmark, but the company had set up excellent examination laboratories at Culham, Oxfordshire, and had established a good reputation. Forensic Alliance had recently been refinanced by Close Brothers Private Equity and it was now competing strongly with the FSS and ourselves in the developing UK market and had opened branches at Risley (near Warrington in Cheshire) and Tamworth (near Birmingham).

It happened that Brian Phillips knew Bill Crossan, who was responsible for Close Brothers' investment in Forensic Alliance, and they had already had discussions about the possibility of LGV acquiring FA. I arranged to go with Brian to see Angela Gallop and Bill Crossan and, having signed a confidentiality agreement in October 2004, we began to explore the possibility of a merger between FA and LGC's forensic division. Brian and Jo Parfrey were convinced of the merit of joining forces to create a significant competitor in the market to the FSS and they made an offer to the FA shareholders in December. The offer was generous – £20 million in cash – far more generous than for any of LGC's previous acquisitions and a reflection, perhaps, more of potential than of FA's performance at the time.

During the due diligence process LGC management (especially Nigel Law and Geoff Battersby) asked many questions and we analysed the rather thin answers given by FA. Because FA had grown rapidly, the accounting was uncertain. Moreover, the relationship with Cellmark was complex and it took us time to uncover that a large chunk of FA's profits arose from the subcontract with Cellmark for DNA work. Although there was no doubt that the acquisition of FA would be a good move from a strategic point of view, and acquiring the company would enable LGC to provide a fully comprehensive service to police forces, LGC management had some real doubts about FA management and the robustness of their business model. LGV were very keen to go ahead, but LGC management had some misgivings and wanted to limit the risk, and insisted on restructuring the offer to include some shares and an 'earn-out'. The new offer was still generous – £15 million upfront and a further £5 million after two years, if modest business projections were met. After further lengthy exchanges, this offer was finally accepted and the acquisition was completed in August 2005. It was funded almost entirely by an increase in our debt with our three banks – HSBC, Société Générale and Bank of Ireland.

There followed a difficult period of integration. LGC and FA had been competitors and the staff in the two organisations (just under 200 in LGC's forensic division and a similar number at FA) were understandably suspicious of one another. The senior management of FA was thin, consisting simply of Angela Gallop (who joined LGC's board) and Tom Palmer, an accountant who looked after all administrative matters at FA and who was about to retire. Unfortunately, below them there was little structure, and Nigel Law asked me to help with an integration plan. In order to determine the future branding of the new business I commissioned some market research from Financial Dynamics which also served to raise awareness of the merger among police forces. I set up various groups to look in detail at how technical teams, safety and quality procedures, human resources etc could best be rationalised and integrated, but progress was slow and often impeded by petty disputes. It transpired that some information about related businesses and their relationship with FA had not been made available during the due diligence process, and LGC management received rather half-hearted support from FA in its efforts to create a single business. The modest synergy savings which had been jointly estimated during the negotiations rapidly turned into substantial additional costs. By early 2006, a new name – LGC Forensics – had been agreed for the new division, but there were many, more intractable, issues that needed to be resolved, and spending seemed impossible to control. The joint business did not initially achieve the agreed business objectives and, as a consequence, the £5 million earn-out component of the deal, due after two years, was not paid. It was the only acquisition that LGC made where the acquired company failed, in this case by a long way, to achieve the agreed targets.

Despite these organisational difficulties, both LGC and FA had won major contracts with the Metropolitan Police and had established an excellent reputation with the largest police service in the UK. We were now being called upon to conduct forensic investigations of major crimes. Our reputation for meticulous investigation also led to work on 'cold cases', serious crimes which had not yet been solved, where we would re-examine evidence, looking for clues which had escaped notice in the original investigation. Among the many crimes that we investigated, LGC Forensics was called upon to re-examine evidence in the high-profile Damilola Taylor case which had already led to two unsuccessful trials. Our painstaking forensic work detected evidential material, including a drop of Damilola's blood found on the heel of a trainer found in the room of one of the suspects and another found on a sweatshirt belonging to another suspect, which had been missed by the FSS scientists who conducted the original forensic examinations. LGC's new evidence led to the conviction of two youths for the dreadful killing of Damilola and brought to an end a very sad case which had deeply troubled the nation. Similarly, LGC Forensics contributed to the reinvestigation of the killing of Rachel Nickell and other high profile cases, and we were called upon to identify the bodies of victims of the London Underground bombings on 7 July 2005. Our Teddington laboratories had expanded and we had invested heavily in examination laboratories and new equipment and techniques to detect minute quantities of DNA.

As with the high-profile work on sheep brains that we had carried out for Defra, we resisted the temptation to seek publicity for our forensic successes. Indeed, I went to see the chairman of the FSS, which had conducted the original forensic work, to assure him that we would not seek to make capital out of the cold case reviews. The original investigations by the FSS were carried out under huge pressure, whereas LGC had much more time to examine items in immense detail using the most up-to-date methods.

Despite our growing scientific reputation in forensic science, and considerable success in helping the police solve cases, LGC's efforts to expand its forensic services in the UK did not go smoothly, and our merger of FA into our new division, LGC Forensics, was plagued with administrative difficulties. By contrast, our move, in accordance with our strategic plan, to establish forensic services outside the UK, though challenging, seemed relatively straightforward. With advice from Uwe de Buhr, who had made contact with justice departments and the police and had received some positive feedback, we decided that we should set up some operations in Germany. We knew that penetrating this market would take time, but we felt LGC would be in a strong position once the German authorities recognised the advantages of private providers.

Having conducted a search for possible acquisitions, we identified two small private companies which we felt could act as the foundation for an expanded operation in Germany. The first was AGOWA GmbH, a small company involved in genetic sequencing, based in Berlin. The company had been founded by a husband and wife team who, it transpired, wanted to retire in order to sail round the world. With Ray Ah-Sun I had discussions with them. Like many owners of small companies, they wanted to be assured that their company would be well looked after, and Uwe helped convince them that the transaction would make sense. The second target was the Institut für Blutgruppenforschung (IFB) in Cologne, again a husband-and-wife-owned company, but specialising in blood tests and paternity testing. I went to Berlin to complete the acquisition of AGOWA in December 2005 and the acquisition of IFB was completed in April 2006. Managing the new acquisitions was not easy and I was pleased and relieved when John McQuillian, who had joined LGC management as director of our life-sciences business, took over the reins. He took immediate charge of these two small companies, made plans for management succession, and set them on the path of growth. I was impressed to meet on the tube one evening one of our able DNA scientists, Lucy Johns, who was busy reading a textbook for the crash course in German she was doing, having been asked by John McQuillian to move from Teddington to Cologne to help manage our new laboratory there.

Our forensics division was not alone in seeking to expand by acquisition. In line with our new strategic plan, our reference standards business, LGC Promochem, also saw the advantage of using acquisitions to expand or diversify its market presence. However, these were smaller, lower-profile, acquisitions in niche areas, which we felt we could build on. In August 2005 we concluded an arrangement with Quality Management Limited (QM)and its subsidiary Aquacheck Limited, companies based in Bury, Lancashire, which provided proficiency testing services to food and environmental laboratories throughout Europe. QM was owned by Antony Meier, whom I got to know and like during our negotiations. Like many other founder owners, he was concerned that his staff should have a good future after his retirement and he felt that LGC would be a suitable home for his business. He liked our culture, professionalism, concern for staff, and attitude to business, and he seemed to identify with our aims. Under the agreed arrangements, LGC acquired 50% of the share capital of these companies with an option (which we exercised) to acquire the remaining 50% a year later. Proficiency testing (where companies are able to compare their performance against other participants in the scheme) is closely linked to the use of reference materials (which allow practitioners to compare their results against a standard). The vision was to create a business providing a full range of services to help laboratories improve and demonstrate the quality of their measurements. In the event, this was a highly successful move and added considerable value to our standards business.

Our overseas expansion had deliberately been strongly focused on Europe. (Our investment in India was part of a joint venture which meant the management task there was shared.) We had considered many times if and how we should approach the US market. I was mindful of how several UK companies (including quite large ones) had burnt their fingers in trying to enter the US and was aware of the investment that would be required. Our initial move was to send an experienced sales manager, Morris Legge, for a one-year secondment to investigate the market for reference materials and other services and to look for a small acquisition which could provide the necessary critical mass for us to launch LGC in North America. Morris spent most of his time visiting companies, but set up a 'virtual office' in Philadelphia which gave LGC an address and access to meeting rooms and was well placed for visits to pharmaceutical companies based along the east coast. (I was impressed by this highly economical office arrangement when I visited.) Our business grew slowly but steadily and subsequently we appointed a full-time manager for the US who began to strengthen our presence. Identifying a company to acquire (and one that wanted to be acquired) was a process which took time and we held back for some time from making a significant investment in the US.

However, despite the undoubted success of LGC Promochem's strategy of European growth, now developing fast, in particular in Eastern Europe, the division suffered a major setback when, without any prior discussion or warning, I received a call from US Pharmacopeia (USP) (the largest producer of pharmacopeia standards) informing me of their intention to terminate our distribution agreement. Although Ray Ah-Sun, Tilo Karrer and Sury Rao (managing director of our Indian joint venture) had made every effort to foster good relations with USP, their quasi-government status and the tension between their public service obligations and commercial aspirations, did not facilitate easy exchanges. Moreover, their two senior managers involved with us were not easy characters. On one occasion Ray and I had flown to Barcelona to meet up with one of them, and had found ourselves having a tense dinner with him; his mood swings, from being kind and considerate one minute to barely concealed anger the next, made doing business difficult. On another occasion I was invited to address USP's annual conference, during which I had a private dinner with the two senior managers and then separate discussions. As on many previous occasions when Ray and I had met them in Washington, we talked about collaboration (USP was very respectful of LGC's science and wanted greater access to it), but I found it hard to fathom where, if anywhere, this was all leading. Now, despite clear assurances that had been given to Brian Phillips during LGV's due diligence process, it was apparent that it was leading nowhere. We managed to negotiate a more ordered termination of our highly profitable distribution agreement than had at first been proposed, but it was some time before we had restructured our business in response to the loss of the USP contract and adapted our business model to place greater weight on manufacturing our own reference materials rather than acting simply as a distributor.

The difficult integration of Forensic Alliance and our other acquisitions put considerable strain on the senior management and I was sad that Nigel Law, my successor as chief executive, and John Mason, with whom I had worked for many years and whom I held in high regard, did not forge a closer working relationship. They had very different attributes and personalities and I had hoped that, with support from Geoff Battersby, who quickly established himself as a dependable finance director, they could provide a strong leadership team, each contributing qualities that the other lacked. However, it did not really work out and because of this, and for personal reasons, John left in April 2006 to pursue a very different career as chief executive of the diocese of Chester. John had played a pivotal role in LGC's development. He had led the Pentagon Programme of culture change and two years earlier had helped rescue the transaction with Legal & General Ventures by conducting a thorough review of the business forecasts. His sober and considered analysis was a useful counterbalance to the exuberance and optimism of others, including me.

In the annual report for 2006, the tenth anniversary of the company's formation, Nigel Law reported a record year; there were now four times as many staff as when the company was formed and there had been a six-fold increase in sales. However, I was worried that, apparently encouraged by Jo Parfrey of LGV, Nigel seemed to be toying with the idea of a profitable early sale of the business to yet another private equity group, and was not devoting the effort I felt was needed to strengthening LGC's management and identifying future areas of growth. With John Mason's departure, insufficient thought was being given to the day-to-day operational aspects of the business as opposed to the more exciting area of deals and acquisitions.

A shock was to follow. I had known for some time that Brian Phillips's relationship with his boss, the head of Legal & General Ventures, Adrian Johnson, was not good and that Brian had on several occasions been on the point of leaving. However, it was still a surprise when Brian told me that he and LGV were agreeing terms and he was to leave immediately. His sudden departure was deeply unsettling. He had taken a keen and personal interest in LGC's development and had been holding out against LGV's early exit, wanting to invest in LGC over a longer period than just two years. Michael O'Donnell, who was nominated by Adrian as Brian's replacement on our board, was keener to examine the immediate sale of

LGC on the back of our excellent 2006 results, and he asked Ian Kent and me to explore the appointment of advisers to assist with a sale. Neither of us was particularly happy with the turn of events at LGV. Nevertheless, Ian and I, admittedly rather reluctantly, embarked on a series of visits to the likes of Lehman Brothers, Credit Suisse, and Rothschild and had discussions with teams who, needless to say, were enthusiastic about the prospect of becoming LGC's corporate finance advisers in anticipation of another major transaction.

While this was going on, in the autumn of 2006, LGC's business started to slow down. Out of the blue LGC received notice that Defra wanted to terminate our contract with them for genotyping sheep as part of the National Scrapie Plan. They emphasised that our performance on this contract had been excellent, but the other contractor's prices were lower and, since the work was likely to decline, they had decided to place all the work with them. Had LGC's managers picked up on this at an earlier stage, LGC might have been able to respond, but the decision had been made and there was nothing that could be done now other than plan for the closure of a capital-intensive laboratory with some excellent staff. Even more worrying was the state of our forensics division. Following the acquisition of Forensic Alliance a year earlier, we had incurred major costs in our attempts to rationalise our forensics work and we had invested substantially in new DNA technology which was taking much longer to introduce than planned. Moreover, the UK forensics market was not opening up as we had hoped and there were major delays in police forces issuing invitations to tender. It transpired that parts of our acquired forensics business were making losses and, despite many exchanges, Nigel Law had still failed to find an accommodation with Orchid Cellmark, to whom the former Forensic Alliance was obliged to subcontract DNA work. Not surprisingly, LGV put a halt to plans to sell LGC, and the business entered a period when it felt as if it was drifting. It became increasingly likely that the drop in profitability would mean that LGC would have difficulty meeting its bank covenants at the end of the year.

With a view to getting things back on track, Michael O'Donnell asked me to take over as chairman of our executive management committee and I immediately instituted a programme to identify economies, mainly in the support services. As previously, we adopted an 'activity value analysis' approach, on this occasion calling on the services of Develin and Partners to help manage the process. However, in spite of a ban on new recruitment, our forensics division, now run by Angela Gallop and an interim manager she and Nigel had appointed, continued to spend money and take on new staff. The seriousness of the situation of failing to meet our bank covenants had simply not registered with some managers. With leveraged private-equity-owned companies the position is black and white. If targets are met, the management is left alone to get on with the job; if targets are not met, even if the company continues to trade profitably and the shortfall is quite small, the investors and banks are unforgiving, particularly if they have not been warned in advance of problems on the horizon.

Moreover, the external financial climate was beginning to change. The re-negotiation of our bank covenants, which under 'normal' circumstances would have been fairly routine, turned out to be a lengthy and costly process. To make matters worse, our defined benefit pension scheme, which many years earlier had been closed to new members, was again forecasting a deficit. The company had already increased individual and company contributions, but the pension scheme's actuarial advisers seemed suddenly to discover that people were living longer, and that the calculations they had made just a year or two earlier now needed to be revised. I have never understood how the actuarial profession is so well paid when there are no consequences for them when they get their calculations spectacularly wrong. Fortunately, the calm and thoughtful approach of the pension fund chairman, Jim Cook, steadied everyone's nerves.

The feeling that the company's growth was slowing down (by comparison with previous continuous expansion) and that our profit margins were under pressure was obviously of concern to LGV, but neither of our non-executive directors, John Stevens and Uwe de Buhr, nor I as deputy chairman, were aware of what they were planning. One morning in December 2006 I received a telephone call from Ian Kent during a break in a meeting he was having at LGV shortly before leaving on a business trip to the US, to say that he would be resigning from the board. I was shocked, not just by the news that LGC was about to lose a chairman who really understood the business and was highly respected by the executive team, but also by the way in which the matter was being handled. LGV's failure to consult members of the board was arrogant and went against the culture of good corporate governance and decency I had worked hard to create. Moreover, it rapidly transpired that LGV had already appointed a new chairman, again without any prior consultation. As majority shareholder, they had the power to do this, but the manner of their actions created bad feeling and suspicion.

I was determined that Ian's departure should be handled properly with appropriate announcements which acknowledged the success of the company during his period as chairman. I also persuaded LGV that he should be allowed to retain the relatively small number of shares he had purchased. (I had never felt that non-executive directors should be allowed large numbers of shares; I was more concerned that staff at all levels, who worked tirelessly for the company, should have a stake.) It was agreed that Ian should resign from the board early in the new year and the new chairman, Stuart Wallis, would be appointed shortly afterwards.

Jacquie and I had arranged a holiday in Brazil in the New Year and it was not possible for me to meet the new chairman until our return towards the end of January. During our holiday I had plenty of time to reflect on the state of LGC, the events which had led up to Ian's departure, and my frustration at seeing Nigel Law failing to get to grips with the management issues. By the time Stuart Wallis and I finally met at our Culham laboratory he had been thoroughly briefed by Nigel and Geoff Battersby and had visited a couple of the company's sites with Nigel. Stuart was an accountant by background but had risen to prominence when he took over as chief executive at the pharmaceutical company Fisons at a time when the company was subject to a takeover. He essentially broke the company up, winning the gratitude of shareholders and making a substantial sum for himself. His reputation as a 'turnaround specialist' was the reason that LGV had appointed him.

As someone whose motivation was building a business, not breaking it up to extract maximum value for shareholders, I was understandably suspicious. However, I tried to keep an open mind and listened to what Stuart had to say. He said that he could sort out the problem we were having with the banks by calling on his good contacts and that he had concluded we needed better management information. In the interests of getting LGC back on track, I offered to return full time, but made it clear that this would not be possible with Nigel continuing as chief executive. Stuart said that he had already decided to replace Nigel with an appointment of his own choice and that finding the right person would not take long. He would consider my offer to return full time on an interim basis.

The board meeting which was held at the end of January was a short and tense affair. Geoff Battersby reported that operating profit for the 9 months until December 2006 was £6.6 million, nearly £3 million behind the budget. The main reason for the variance was a substantial shortfall in LGC Forensics, the division formed after our acquisition of Forensic Alliance and led by their former chief executive, Angela Gallop. Stuart Wallis ended the meeting by presenting his priorities: increasing profitability, sorting out the banking, resolving the pension deficit problem, improving management information, and changing the structure and management. During the next couple of weeks, I got to know a little more about Stuart and his approach. He had agreed to purchase 25,000 shares from LGV at their initial value of £1. This price was much lower than the price agreed for the small number of transactions over the previous year with staff shareholders, and did not reflect the profitable and successful record of the business since 2004. The transaction was a matter between LGV and the chairman, but I found it distasteful.

Stuart Wallis decided to take up my offer to return to running the company as interim chief executive but made clear this would not be for long, and he arranged for Nigel Law to leave. Although Nigel departed early in March with very favourable terms, the period was horrible for all concerned. Moreover, on taking over the reins again, albeit temporarily, I set myself a tough agenda. My first priority was to cut £1.5 million from costs and that inevitably meant reducing the number of staff. Within three weeks of taking over again, I had pressed ahead with 50 redundancies. Much earlier in my career I had been responsible for making redundancies and I had hated it. This time it was particularly hard to say goodbye to staff in the company I had created, where such emphasis was put on staff welfare.

The second major task was to sort out LGC Forensics. The main issue was the quality of management at all levels. I immediately appointed headhunters to identify suitable candidates for a managing director and head of sales, but I also initiated changes at much lower levels. It was revealing to visit the laboratories at Culham, accompanied by the leader of our process modelling team, and see how some of the working practices were dreadfully inefficient. I set up pilot improvement schemes within some of the sections of the divisions, such as forensic toxicology, where the local managers had simply not been given the tools to improve their operations and where simple, often inexpensive, changes could lead to major improvements in productivity.

However, although the problems with LGC Forensics primarily boiled down to management, the delay in the long-awaited opening up of the forensic science market continued to be a major issue. I felt LGC needed to press its case at a senior level in police forces and within government and I turned to the PR company, Financial Dynamics, who had helped us on previous occasions, to develop a plan. This involved commissioning a study from an independent consultancy, Europe Economics, on the competition aspects of the market. The study concluded that a market which had previously been dominated by a monopoly supplier (the Forensic Science Service) was moving towards a 'monopsonistic' market, one with a very few dominant customers, groups of police forces who had decided to pool their procurement. Our intention was to use this report to help us in lobbying for more sensible changes in the market which I felt could only arise if there were better political understanding of the issues.

The third task was to try to motivate staff, who were acutely aware of the changes at the top and the uncertainty created by our below-budget trading position. I embarked on a series of visits to all sites where I addressed staff and explained the position, emphasising the opportunities open to the company and how we were addressing them. This gave impetus to my final and substantial task which was to develop a strategic plan which would look beyond our immediate problems and set out objectives for the coming few years.

Obviously I had to explain to the banks what I was doing, and I was able to call on my long and excellent relationship with HSBC to buy a little time while the company was brought back on track. Geoff Battersby patiently renegotiated the terms of our debt and, within three months of my taking over again as chief executive, things were looking brighter.

Not unreasonably, our new chairman wanted to clear the decks as far as possible in the accounts for 2006/7 and, in addition to making provision for the cost of redundancies associated with my restructuring programme, we decided to write off goodwill of £11.6 million associated with our acquisition in the previous year of Forensic Alliance Limited. For the first time in ten years we reported a drop in our trading profit.

Although it became clear that the appointment of a new chief executive would take rather longer than initially expected (the headhunters Egon Zehnder had now been appointed) I had no idea how long my interim period as chief executive would last. However, I threw myself into the task of sorting things out and enjoyed it. What I did not enjoy was my relationship with the new chairman. Stuart and I had very little in common; I was interested in the business, its customers and its staff; his unambiguous aim was to make money and then depart.

During the summer of 2007 I met some of the candidates for the post of new chief executive who had been suggested by Egon Zehnder and interviewed by Michael O'Donnell and Stuart. With the exception of a rather interesting, but inexperienced, candidate, they failed to impress. I pressed ahead with preparing a new strategic plan which aimed further to strengthen LGC's vision as a leading science-based service company setting standards in analytical science. Some spadework had already been done on this in separate plans which each division had drawn up. However, these tended to be 'wish lists' and I felt it was important for me to set out the overall strategic direction and to consider major issues, such as geographical spread, the rationalisation of sites, and acquisitions policy, which had to be considered at corporate, rather than divisional, level. The plan identified areas with significant growth potential, including India and China, and put forward proposals for rationalisation of our multiple sites in the UK. It placed emphasis on employee involvement, in line with my view that LGC would only be able to retain a distinctive position if staff felt proud of their company. It was the 'big picture', rather than a collection of divisional proposals and showed how LGC could more than double in size within a five-year period.

My plan, with its proposals for yet again transforming LGC, was ambitious, but underlying it were some fundamental issues concerning LGC's business model. Much of what LGC did, the provision of services, was not itself particularly entrepreneurial. Up to now LGC's success had been based on spotting new scientific applications or new market opportunities and being seen as taking the lead in the application of new methodology. It was a relatively small group of my colleagues who were constantly considering such innovations. From the many seeds planted, only a few germinated, and only a few of these grew into trees. I had encouraged some ideas which initially appeared unpromising, and we had pursued opportunities in genotyping, BSE testing, proficiency testing, and reference materials which had in time developed into substantial businesses. Obviously, LGC was now of a size when profitability could be improved through efficiency and good husbandry, but if the company were to continue to grow in the way it had done in the previous decade, it needed to foster an entrepreneurial approach, encouraging ideas and looking for new areas which would replace some of those which were now maturing and would be more exposed to competition. New business opportunities in areas such as security, medical services, laboratory standards and genetic sequencing would be needed to replace areas likely to reduce, such as BSE testing and even forensic science services in the UK, where, although LGC was expanding its market share, the overall market was likely to be static or even to decline in the medium term. LGC did not want to present itself as engaged in routine 'testing'; rather, it needed to select areas where it could use science to solve problems. The trick would be to spot new scientific opportunities which we could develop in markets in which we had become established. While acquisitions would no doubt play a part in achieving future growth, they carried risk. Up to now, our most successful acquisitions had been small and carefully targeted to allow us to develop new areas more rapidly. Although larger acquisitions had their attraction, they inevitably carried greater risk. I did not believe that, on their own, they represented a sensible strategy for LGC.

In this context, it is interesting to consider how private companies are valued. Whereas publicly quoted companies have a market value (reflected in their share price), the value of private companies can only really be assessed when they are sold. In considering the value of a company, before making an offer to acquire it for example, financial investors often use a benchmark based on multiples of their much-loved measure, EBITDA. EBITDA (earnings before interest, taxes, depreciation and amortisation) is a measure of cash generation capability; investments in fixed and working capital, as well as payment of taxes and interest are excluded. The multiple of EBITDA used in the calculation of value varies according to the sector of industry the company is in. When LGV invested in LGC their offer represented a multiple of about 8x, which was similar to that used in our offer to acquire Forensic Alliance. However, in all other acquisitions that LGC made, our offer represented a much lower multiple of EBITDA. When LGV finally exited, the multiple was considerably higher. Of course, much depends on whether the EBITDA data used is historical or based on future projections, and how far the buyer trusts the data. In the end, the value of a company comes down to what is agreed between the buyer and the seller. The buyer may be prepared to pay more if he perceives a rosy future for the acquired business; the seller may be prepared to accept less if he feels that other interests (such as the protection of staff) are better satisfied. Many studies have shown that acquisitions do not always add value; in other words, the value of a combined company is not necessarily higher than that of the component parts. The challenge is that acquisitions are often opportunistic, yet they need to be considered as part of a strategic plan. Price is probably less important than getting the right fit, but paying a lower price obviously reduces exposure to risk. Some companies have been highly successful in using acquisitions to develop their business; in other cases acquisitions have been disastrous failures. My view was that acquisitions would help LGC develop further, but they needed to be coupled with entrepreneurial business development from within the existing organisation.

As with the corporate plan that we had prepared six years earlier, I saw staff 'engagement' as the key to achieving the company's new objectives and creating new business opportunities. There were now well over a thousand staff in the company, and linking their individual aims and aspirations with the company's overall objectives presented a challenge. I spent time looking at how companies in 'employer of the year' competitions were managed and how some technology companies managed to stay entrepreneurial even when they had grown into large corporations. I looked at how staff attitudes, as measured in the regular surveys we undertook, had changed, and considered the potential for IT to revolutionise the way we provided services to our customers. I was convinced that a stimulating, creative and enjoyable workplace environment would have a direct influence on LGC's future performance. The Pentagon Programme had now run its course, but a new programme for renewing the company was essential. This had to be at the heart of any new plan. When I presented my plan to the board in November 2007, it was endorsed without qualification, but there was very little discussion. How different from the board which Ian Kent had chaired, which would have closely questioned, and had a lively and constructive debate on, all aspects of the strategy. Although John Stevens and Uwe de Buhr had points to make, there was no longer anyone on the board who had a real understanding of the business other than from a purely financial perspective.

After the meeting, Geoff Battersby and I met the candidate who was to be appointed as the next chief executive. A qualified accountant who had previously worked for British Airways, National Air Traffic Services and Hays, David Richardson had taken over as chief executive of British Mediterranean Airlines, a small franchise airline, in very difficult circumstances. He had managed to protect the shareholders by selling the airline to BMI and was now looking for a new opportunity.

I was pleased that during the nine months that I had acted as interim CEO, I had managed to get the company back on track and LGC was already looking in much better shape. I had appointed new management for LGC Forensics, I had rescued an acquisition in Germany for LGC Standards which had been off the rails, I had cut costs (and, regrettably, staff), I had helped Geoff achieve new agreements with our banks, and I had agreed with DTI a process for the replacement of John Marriott on his retirement as Government Chemist. Most important, LGC's trading was reviving, with the delayed opportunities for contracts with the police now looking much more promising. So, although I was sad to retire from LGC, I was pleased to be able to leave the company in excellent shape, with plenty of opportunities in the pipeline, and a strategic plan which showed the way to a new phase of development and growth.

At my final board meeting on 27 November 2007 John Stevens was kind enough to record that the LGC Group owed its existence to me, and that 'the company's vitality, success and reputation were attributable to

Richard's vision and leadership'. He noted that the Entrepreneur of the Year Award I had received in 2003 had reflected my business success in creating wealth and jobs both nationally and internationally. My handover to David Richardson went easily and I held a reception for staff in our restaurant in Teddington just before Christmas, before finally clearing my desk and retiring from LGC.

The board hosted a reception for me in February 2008, to which many of the people with whom I had had contact and done business were invited. It was a very happy occasion involving people from all over the world and from the very many organisations I had dealt with over the years. I was particularly pleased that the event was held in the Apothecaries' Hall, the third occasion on which LGC had met there for a celebration.

I had not appreciated until I retired from LGC what a weight I had been carrying for so many years. Suddenly, most of this weight was lifted, although I remained available for advice and, of course, I remained the largest shareholder apart from LGV. I had left LGC in very good shape; our 2008 accounts reported that turnover was level and that profit declared in the accounts was down less than expected from the previous year, despite some significant provisions, including for the pension fund. And there were now some new juicy fruits ready to be harvested. I was able to reflect with pride on what I had achieved.

Although I had retired from LGC feeling pleased that the company was set fair, there was one matter which left a bad taste. At the AGM in September 2007 shareholders had been asked to agree that the holding company should cease to be a public limited company (plc) and revert to being a limited company. I had expressed reservations about this change at the board, but it had been pushed through by the chairman and LGV on the grounds that it would simplify administration. Almost as soon as I had left, my former colleagues told me that the chairman was on the brink of buying a large number of shares out of the reserve that we had made available for new senior staff and others. I was told that this deal was about to be settled outside the board. This action went completely against the governance structure which I had created and the culture of reasonable pay and reward that I had tried to foster. I thought long and hard before deciding to write to the board, explaining why I had put such emphasis on good corporate governance, and explaining that LGC's ethos had been built on a high degree of trust between management and staff, reflected in the 'values' which had been adopted by the company. I noted that allocating additional shares to non-executive directors had not been mentioned at the last AGM and that not to declare this proposal at the meeting was contrary to LGC's 'values', and economical with the truth, since a specific question on the subject had been asked by a staff shareholder. I noted that shareholders had been asked at the AGM to delegate to the board responsibility in relation to the new tranche of shares and that they had agreed this, trusting that the full board would consider any new share allocations in a serious and measured way. My letter caused a stir but the purchase of a further 16,900 shares, for a price of just £1 per share, by the chairman, made more palatable no doubt by allocations to the rest of the board, was authorised. Within less than two years, the value of these shares, now several million pounds, would be realised, a huge capital gain with virtually zero risk to those who benefited.

One task I completed shortly after I left was helping with the appointment of a new Government Chemist to succeed John Marriott who had taken over the position from me in 2002 and was now approaching retirement. Under the arrangements I had agreed when the company was formed in 1996, the appointment (which carried an honorarium of £10 a year) was still made by the Secretary of State, despite the fact that the person appointed had also to be a director of LGC's UK trading company. The appointment procedure had been changed to comply with the Nolan principles of openness and transparency and the DTI arranged for the post to be advertised. I was asked to join David Evans, a senior civil servant, and Elizabeth Llewellyn-Smith, the retired head of St Hilda's College, Oxford and an independent civil service appointment assessor on the panel which interviewed the six short-listed candidates. I was delighted when the panel agreed unanimously that Dr Derek Craston, who had been with LGC since 1991, should be appointed the new Government Chemist.

After I retired from LGC I decided to sever most of my links with the company and to do other things – becoming chairman of a fascinating start-up company, doing some consultancy, playing my violin, and pursuing joint interests with Jacquie. However, still a major shareholder,

I was pleased to be kept up to date on progress and delighted to hear that all LGC divisions were doing well. Over the next year the trading position continued to improve. The purchase of a reference materials supplier in Germany was completed and LGC made a couple of small acquisitions to strengthen LGC Forensics' capability in digital forensics. It came as no surprise to hear during 2009 that the consultants, KPMG, had been appointed to manage the sale of the company. The process ended in a last-minute bidding contest between two private equity firms and in February 2010 it was announced that the company was to be sold to Bridgepoint for £257 million. A month after this announcement the transaction was completed. I was now able to sell the shares which I had purchased in 2004 (when 3i sold their stake and LGV became the majority owner) with some of the proceeds from my original investment in 1996 when we had remortgaged our house. I had recovered my initial investment many, many times over, giving Jacquie and me financial security for the rest of our lives and allowing us to set up a charitable trust to support a number of causes important to us. The transaction allowed a sizeable payment to be made to cover the deficit in the staff pension scheme, and payments were again made to all staff under a 'phantom share scheme' which John Mason and I had established shortly after LGV's investment and which was partly funded from the employee benefit trust I had established at the outset in 1996. After just two years, the chairman, Stuart Wallis, departed and the new owners, Bridgepoint, replaced him with Graham Love, formerly chief executive of Qinetic. David Richardson continued as chief executive.

When I look back at LGC's genesis and consider its evolution, I have no doubt that the company benefited from being privately owned, with staff as shareholders and generally supportive private equity investors, rather than being a listed company subject to shorter-term pressures. My experience of private equity, though mostly favourable, was mixed. Partly because they were minority shareholders, 3i were generally a hands-off investor and I was given almost total freedom to develop the company in the way I saw fit. The involvement of staff as shareholders facilitated fundamental changes and created an ethos in which mutual respect, engagement and enthusiasm were key elements. My initial experience with our second private equity investor, Legal & General Ventures, who became majority shareholder, was excellent. Their managing director responsible for LGC was imaginative and constructive, and he was a valuable source of advice based on experience of investing in many different types of companies. However, his departure saw a change in approach, and the less creative and more self-interested aspects of private capital came to the surface. Of course investors want a return on their investment, but focusing on short-term gains can be damaging to the longer-term growth of a company. Generally, and not specifically in relation to LGC, one consequence of this trend is that leaders who have an intuitive feel for their companies, and who have a natural connection with customers and staff, have been replaced by impersonal managers, who instantly respond to investors and accountants but have no real affinity with their business.

Although privately owned, LGC benefited, I believe, from having a board which was structured in the same way as the boards of publicly owned companies, with an independent non-executive chairman and other non-executive directors. As chief executive, I was fully responsible for the direction and management of the company, and I had strong views on how I wanted 'my' company to develop. However, I felt it was important that new ideas were tested and challenged by the board, and that there were proper procedures in place to ensure accountability of financial and business decisions, and independent checks on the appointment and reward of staff. In such a board, the relationship between the chief executive and chairman is crucial. There has to be openness, trust, and a sense of common purpose, but the relationship should not become so close that independent judgement is compromised. During the five years that Ian Kent was chairman, we worked well together. Ian was certainly challenging, sometimes even combative, but I valued his opinions highly. He was creative but also a stickler for good governance. We frequently had lively discussions at our board meetings, with non-executives contributing strongly and asking searching questions of the executives, but we always seemed to be able to resolve differences without resorting to a vote. After Legal & General Ventures became the majority shareholder, the situation changed in that LGV had the power to override the board should they wish to do so. Their initial representative, Brian Phillips, was pro-active, in particular in relation to our acquisition of Forensic

Alliance, and took a very close interest in the progress of the business, but he always respected the position of the board. His departure heralded a different regime and, to my enormous regret, the character of the board changed radically. Clearly there are many different approaches to running companies, and a strong chief executive has the greatest influence on a company's success. However, I remain convinced of the merits of combining entrepreneurial leadership with good corporate governance. The culture created by this will influence for the good the direction of the whole organisation.

I have often reflected on the tension between 'reasonable' reward and incentivisation. I was repulsed by the 'fat cat' salaries paid to managers in privatised utility companies and the huge bonuses paid in the financial sector to managers who invested other people's money, taking no real risk with their own. I regret the steady increase there has been in the disparity of earnings between those running companies and those working within them. I tried to limit the pay of LGC's top managers (including my own), taking the view that, since they were offered shares or share options in the company, they would receive a reward from LGC's long-term success and could not expect to receive huge salaries as well. I recognise, of course, that many people, particularly in sales roles, are motivated by financial reward, even though others work hard whatever the reward because they enjoy or believe in what they are doing. Any reward system has to be a compromise between the need to incentivise some and fairness for others. The share and bonus schemes which we introduced at all levels aimed to be proportionate and 'fair', in so far as any reward system can be. I was pleased that all staff benefited from the sale of shares when LGV took over from 3i and again when Bridgepoint took over from LGV. Where managers are genuine entrepreneurs, taking risks with their own money and lives, high rewards may be justified, but high pay for relatively secure jobs (with generous compensation if things do not work out) seems to me to be wrong. Greed is unattractive; creating lasting wealth for all through effort and imagination is admirable.

Although LGC's success can be attributed largely to the imagination and hard work of the company's managers and staff, I was fortunate to start it up and develop it during a period which was particularly favourable for technology-based companies. The Labour government between 1997 and 2010 is currently being criticised for its management of the economy; however, the late 1990s and early 2000s was in fact a period when interest rates were steady, taxation for entrepreneurs was very favourable, government spending on science rose substantially in real terms, and there was encouragement for investment in technology through R&D tax credits and regional assistance. LGC benefited from the benign economic conditions which prevailed, and from the measures introduced by Gordon Brown when he was Chancellor of the Exchequer to support innovation and entrepreneurship. Regional assistance in the Northwest and R&D tax credits did not change our strategy, but certainly helped in the early stages of new ventures. However, while the ready availability of debt finance was advantageous to LGV's leveraged investment in 2004, servicing this debt, which had been increased for the acquisition of Forensic Alliance, put strains on LGC in 2006/7 as the banking crisis loomed. Even though LGC's debt was not excessive by industry standards, the strains imposed as a result of a drop in profits, caused regrettable fallout. The gung-ho approach of investors and banks in the early years of the century has now given way to a period when debt finance for entrepreneurial companies is hard to obtain. It would certainly be harder for LGC to develop as rapidly and successfully as it did, if it were starting out on its path today.

I feel I have been incredibly fortunate to have been given the opportunity to set up, develop, mould, and run a company to which I devoted an important part of my life. Little did I expect when I joined the DTI as chief executive of the Laboratory of the Government Chemist Executive Agency that I would be preparing the Agency for privatisation and then bidding against others to buy it. The company I formed provided a wonderful vehicle for me to pursue exciting entrepreneurial ventures, applying scientific ideas in new markets. Throughout my time leading the company I had formed, my energies were focused on profitable growth and creating a successful international enterprise. My determination to retain core values of public service and to apply science for the benefit of society, had elements of 'social enterprise', involving all staff at all levels. I certainly relished the opportunity to create a working environment which reflected some of my own beliefs and values and which I hope the vast majority of staff found inclusive and fun.

Index

Index